Rhinoceros Zen

Zen Martial Arts and the Path to Freedom

by Jeffrey M. Brooks

Illustrations by Tarleton Reynolds Brooks

A Publication of

Bronx, NY

A Publication of

FIGHTINGARTS.**com**

A division of eCommunities LLC

Bronx, NY

http://www.fightingarts.com

(718) 549-2151

http://www.fightingarts.com
invites the reader to visit our site to read articles by
Jeff Brooks and other authors on a wide variety
of martial arts and related subjects, to join in our active
forums, and to purchase other books, videos, CDs and
other products of interest from our Internet store.

Acknowledgements

Bringing this book to fruition has been a collaborative effort. To the millennia of masters, teachers, and practitioners, known and unknown, go the lion's share of gratitude. I did not make up the stuff that really matters in this book.

Thanks go to the thousands of people with whom I have shared training and experience in this life. I am indebted to the tough, accomplished and generous teachers I have learned from and practiced with: Nagamine Shoshin, Sakiyama Sogen, Fujita Issho, Shinzato Katsuhiko and Michael Roach; to Phil Zaleski; Doug Sloan; Nick Racanelli; to all the people around the world who put their lives on the line for others; to Christopher Caile for bringing a broad, knowledgeable and sincere voice to a corner of the world that has sorely needed one; and to Tarleton—to whom every word is dedicated.

Foreword

By Christopher Caile

I was extremely pleased at the prospect of publishing Jeff Brooks' new book: *Rhinoceros Zen - Zen Martial Arts and the Path to Freedom.*

I have published his work many times before. His articles on Zen and the Martial Arts on the site I founded, FightingArts.com, have become favorites with readers. The articles are always overflowing with insight, providing unique ways to view karate, kata, Zen, practice and practitioners' continuing struggles to plumb the depths of their lives and their practice. I knew immediately that this new book would find a large audience, an audience drawn from all walks of life.

I was right. This book will careen around your mind, illuminate unquestioned beliefs and perhaps even prompt you to take a fresh look at your path and your values—even to recognize the unlimited possibilities that constitute you.

This is no dry philosophical tome—it is a wild ride: a fun read, insightful and fascinating.

From chapter to chapter, Brooks draws the reader down the zigzag path of his life and studies, a path of discipline and continual search. Each chapter is a separate colorful vignette, lively and crisp, with lessons and insights served up in bite-sized chunks, easy to digest. And there are many different courses that contribute to this tasty feast.

If Zen itself were not a big enough topic, Brooks spices his brew with experience, philosophy and insight drawn from his second life discipline: karate. The two disciplines are presented side by side throughout - one seemingly quiet and inner, the other active and external, contrasting yet complementary too. But in Brooks' mind they are one - like two pieces of a broken mirror that shimmer with their own reflections, but both representing the same light but reflected differently. Brooks shows how both disciplines explore fundamental questions of how to live, how to end suffering and how to remake the self.

Using this experience Brooks guides the reader along his or her own path toward choosing a coherent life in the modern, fragmented world. He delves into the importance of creating a life of practice, something that includes both disciplined effort and moral direction, and that can transform and train people to do good and avoid suffering.

But the reader should be warned not to look for some logical argued theme or linear presentation that builds toward conclusion. Subjects, stories, observations and lessons, change and mix, each page turning into new surprises—juxtapositions that mix, blend, and contrast, each layer presenting another facet or reflection of insight taken from Brooks' life, Zen or the Martial Arts. It's a collage of first hand experience that plunges the reader directly into a world of experience all their own.

Perhaps Brooks' most special gift is his ability to translate the sophisticated, abstract and complex into words and stories that the layman can appreciate and absorb. Few individuals have this talent, but when found they are celebrated. Immediately coming to mind would be luminaries such as Stephen W. Hawking in physics, Carl Sagan the astronomer and Joseph Campbell who brought mythology to life. Zen and the martial arts have also had their own translators -- people who have enlivened and popularized their subjects. They include Eugene Herrigel, author of *Zen in the Art of Archery*, Donn Draeger with his pioneering in-depth studies of Japanese and other martial arts, as well as Dave Lowry, whose books and articles spill over with insightful explorations of the subtleties of the martial arts and ways.

Jeff Brooks in his *Rhinoceros Zen* may provide just such a landmark—something that not only brings to life his subjects, but that also distills from their insights a deeper understanding of human nature and action.

Thus, in this book, Brooks mimics life. His messages build and impact the way we experience life, as events and experiences over time shape our own selves, actions and attitudes. When finished the reader is left with a different way of viewing and perceiving life and the many internal and external battles that shape our existence.

Contents

Acknowledgements   iii

Foreword   iv

Introduction   1

1. The Mysterious Package   4
2. In a Heartbeat   9
3. Dot Head   13
4. The Shield   16
5. Okinawa   20
6. Many Mansions   33
7. Sherlock's Craft   36
8. Door Number One   39
9. The Human Realm   41
10. Pen & Sword   48
11. The Investigation   49
12. Our Lord   54
13. Debbie's Boast   57
14. Ten Years of Sweat   60
15. One Light   69
16. Severe Training   73
17. Two Truths   76
18. Five Dollars   80
19. The Hells   85
20. Nothing to Lose   86
21. Welcome to Purgatory   89
22. Kata   92

23. Unwrapping the Mysterious Package   93

24. Every Move You Make   95

25. The Music of Purgatory   100

26. Pet or Meat?   103

27. Wild Life   106

28. Mirror of Mind   109

29. Come Together   114

30. The Sopranos   121

31. The Parts of a Person   124

32. A Day's Work   127

33. What's Going On   134

34. A Dojo   138

35. The Crucible of Karma   145

36. The Alchemy of Action   153

37. The Old Mill   154

38. Innocence & Experience   159

39. The Thrills of Purgatory   161

40. Initiation   166

41. The Nature of a Cup   172

42. Bodhisattvas in the Diamond Net   175

43. Arms and the Man   192

44. The Monk with the Woman in his Arms   194

45. Okinawa in the Ocean of Time   206

46. Sakiyama's Silence   219

47. Double Illumination   220

48. Door Number Two   227

49. Intelligent Body, Strong Mind   229

50. Honest Action   232

51. Kurosawa's Craft   237

52. Forging Body & Mind   241

53. Maximum Killing Power   244

54. From the Shadows   246

55. Doing Right   248

56. Impermanence   251

57. The Sign   257

58. The Bell   259

59. First, Be Not a Jerk   261

60. The Myth of the Privileged Frame   264

61. Sakiyama's Letter   267

62. Beyond the Art of the Deal   269

63. The Threshold   272

64. Grasping   273

65. Rigorous Reflection   276

66. The Contents of the Mysterious Package   278

67. Entering the Stream   279

68. Coming About   281

69. In the Stream   282

70. The Genjo Kata   283

Conclusion: *Why everyone needs a practice*   285

Glossary   290

Author Biography   299

Note on The Artwork   300

By nature people are nearly alike.

By practice they become vastly different.

—Confucius

Introduction

Human kindness is as much a necessity for people as food and water. In places where there is drought or famine people suffer and die. In regions of the world where human kindness is lacking human culture becomes toxic. People suffer and die.

As modern people we often find ourselves in toxic cultural environments. We may enjoy the wonderful advances in science, medicine, education, culture and other areas, but at the same time we often suffer from the unintended consequences of these very innovations. If we are not mindful of the dangers they pose we

can easily succumb, spending too much of our lives in cars, in air
conditioning, in front of the television and computer, bombarded
by media.

Many people feel their lives are slipping by, stuck in unfulfilling
jobs or harmful relationships. We want to do more—be a hero to
our family, achieve something great—without really knowing how
to make it happen. We may feel like we are on a treadmill, busy,
but without a clear idea of where we're going... hoping soon, if
we just keep moving, something better will appear. Even with our
lives outwardly in order, we may still feel a sense of dislocation:
disconnection from the natural world, from a broad community of
shared life, from our own bodies, and from meaningful purpose.

Attempting to accommodate the demands of the modern world
naturally makes us feel hurried, pressured, anxious and unhappy.

And yet streams of wisdom are flowing nearby, all the
time. There are ways, right at hand, by which we can overcome
unhappiness and have the life we want. Whichever path to freedom
we take, we can only overcome our own difficulties by dedication
to self-mastery in the service of others. This book describes how it
can be done. The method is universal; the stories that illustrate it are
personal.

In the early Buddhist literature there is a short poem called the
Rhinoceros Sutra. In it the Buddha compares the characteristics of a
practitioner on the path to freedom to the attributes of a rhinoceros.
They are willing to go it alone. They do not chase anything. They

fear nothing. They simply proceed step by step. When provoked they respond vigorously. When the disturbance is gone, they go on their way.

As practitioners on the path to freedom from suffering we must understand this: if we fail to cultivate our life, like a garden neglected, whatever happens, happens. Left to chance it will grow wild - no food, no flowers, just weeds. We can't thrive on weeds. Our minds, our bodies, our lives are the same way. If we want good results we have to cultivate them. Daily cultivation of the human mind and body is "having a practice."

In this book when I talk about Zen I am talking about Zen as practice, as mind training, as life training. Not as a religious persuasion, not as a set of beliefs incompatible with one's religious or personal worldview, but as an approach to life which, while drawing on a rich tradition of Buddhist philosophy and experience, opens the door to a deeper richness of life for all of us.

1. The Mysterious Package

Having a practice as part of your life is essential.

Embroidered in gold thread in Chinese characters on the black belts worn in our school are the words *Oku myo zai ren shin*. The words mean "Deep reality appears through training the heart and mind."

I received a black belt with these words embroidered on it one day in the winter of 1995. A small package wrapped in brown paper arrived in the mail. I recognized the return address and the handwriting. The package was from Okinawa, sent by Sogen

Sakiyama Roshi, Abbot of Kozenji Zen Temple in Shuri Village. It came as a complete surprise, but one that was perfectly timed.

I had been corresponding with Sakiyama Roshi frequently since I visited his temple the year before. He was a long-time practitioner of Okinawan karate and had been a Zen priest for fifty years. Every day for those fifty years he had led the austere life of a real practitioner.

His letters to me were filled with kind encouragement but often contained criticism as well: direct, forceful and accurate. It was his duty to urge practitioners on. To harder practice. To deeper insight. Compelled by his vows and the role he had taken on he warned me and others of the danger of complacency, of seeking refuge in worldly comforts that dissipate our energy and pull us from the path of practice. I appreciated his effort, even when it hurt my legs—in long hours of seated meditation—or my pride—when I was sure my understanding was correct and he dismissed it with a wave or a shout or the clang of his ear-splitting bell.

I was not at all sure what to expect as I opened the package he sent me. But I was delighted when, pulling the string off the brown paper package, tearing away the bright Okinawan floral stamps, I took out a thick black belt—with the mysterious Chinese characters embroidered in gold thread on the end.

There was a note with it. His message hit home.

He said he had complete confidence in me. I needed that vote of confidence right then, because with great effort I had, just a few days before, managed to break free of Purgatory.

Most everyone's been in 'Purgatory' at some point. It may be an oppressive job, a bad relationship, an injury or an illness. Maybe you got yourself into it by your own choice, thinking it would be okay for a while but then somehow got stuck. My Purgatory took the form of a karate school where I trained for a few years.

Here's what we have to know: these purgatories hold a mirror up to the flaws in our own nature. It is useful to ask ourselves what drew us to these places and people in the first place. What holds us there? Sometimes, just by freeing ourselves of our own flaws, we can be free of oppressive outer circumstances. Sometimes we can find assistance.

At the time I received the black belts from Sakiyama Roshi it had been 12 years since I naively and willingly entered Purgatory. I set aside my good judgment, again and again. People like me, inclined to begin a spiritual practice or a martial art, were often inspired by idealized stories from books and movies. If you rely on idealized stories, hope for the best, and don't heed the signals, you get what's coming to you.

The ideal I sought did not match the reality I found. But obstinately I proceeded.

During the five years I spent in Purgatory I operated under some assumptions, taken on faith, about the nature of martial arts and spiritual practice: that they would inevitably lead to the perfection of the practitioner; and about my own investment of time and money and energy: that they could not be wasted. I wanted my intuition to be right and my investments to pay off. But my hopes, and the philosophical assumptions and practical choices that flowed from them, proved wrong, in spite of how convenient and how wonderful it would have been had they been true.

At a certain point, just a few days before receiving Sakiyama Roshi's package, I said enough is enough.

It was just about this time that a friend of mine returned from a trip to his ancestors' home on the Sioux reservation out west. He had performed the Sun Dance.

It is an ancient Sioux ritual conducted once in four years. Pegs about the size of carpenter's pencil are tied to a post—the Sun Tree—with long strips of hide. These pegs are inserted through small cuts in the skin of the Sun Dancer. Tethered, he begins to dance. As his dance becomes more vigorous and ecstatic the pegs burst from the skin. Painfully, attachment by attachment, he frees himself from his bonds.

Why would this man put himself through something like that? Why have Sioux men done it generation after generation for centuries? Why do any of us willingly take on painful challenges? Living outside the traditional cultures that built these practices, how well can we know what we are getting into?

For me a day came in the winter of 1995 when the last peg ripped free. I had a conversation with the Boss. Walking down a crammed Manhattan avenue, I had the idea that it was my responsibility to tell him the truth no one else was willing to tell.

I told him that what he was teaching had become shallow. While all the members of his karate school had grown as practitioners—under his leadership—he insisted on repeating the same old beginner stuff. Many people were now chafing at being told that it was heretical and personally disloyal for them to continue to learn from sources other than him, while he refused or was unable to teach any more. And the ones who weren't chafing were becoming complacent, and so were declining as practitioners. People were being pressured to give large donations of money. The ideal of tribal loyalty was being substituted for the ideal of perfection through practice. The idealism and excitement of the place was dissolving. I hoped he would understand that I was saying this in the spirit of collaboration and aid. He needed to get the message that something had to be done before it was too late.

He said, "Get on board or get lost." I said, "goodbye."

Now it was up to me. It left me with nothing but genuine practice and the pursuit of honest human relationships, as I made my way as a practitioner.

Sakiyama Roshi, from across the Pacific, understood what I was aiming at. And he completely supported it. And his affirmation echoed across an ocean and a continent as I wound the black belt he sent me around my waist and pulled the knot tight.

2. In a Heartbeat

When fulfilling our worldly aspirations really gets demanding it's easy to seek solace in what we might think of as "a simpler path." The danger is then that while we are pretending to be sort of Amish we may in fact be just giving up. It takes skill and effort to become a decent human being. But how do you set your feet on the right path?

Although it was just an activity at first, I wanted to be serious about practice. Looking back I can see that the seeds of an aspiration to practice were planted when I was young.

When I was 11 I practiced judo at the YMCA. I did not know how to be good at it and since the class was just one hour each Saturday morning for six weeks I wasn't much better at it at the end of the session than I was at the beginning. But the teacher sure looked cool doing it.

My sixth grade teacher was a beatnik. I was 12. She was pretty and wore black turtlenecks and tight skirts and high boots, had straight dark hair parted in the middle and drove a VW bus. She was the ideal woman. On her desk between carved bookends were some books not for us but only for her. There was one book I liked the look of and I often picked it up. The covers were gray. The book had little cartoons of monks—monks on a mountainside, monks with bundles on their backs, monks crossing streams, and monks walking on muddy roads. It had little cryptic poems, four or five brief lines of type. Incomprehensible to me, but they seemed they would reveal something, if I could ever understand them. That teacher saw me staring at them. She said, "You'll never understand that."

As she said this, another little fellow in the class came over and said that she should wear a cross-your-heart bra. "Suddenly you're shapelier," he said. It was a line of copy from an ad that was on TV in those days. I was amazed. I would never be able to say a thing like that to a teacher. I did not think I would ever be able to say something like that, ever. But I was sure that, at least, I could understand the little book. I wanted her to know. Thirty years later I found a copy of the very same little book, in a church basement book sale. Like seeing a friend who looks so much older but in some ways, hasn't changed at all.

When I was 14, I was in my room one afternoon doing my homework when my Mom called out that Richie was downstairs. She said he didn't feel like coming up, so I should go down. That was unusual because when my friends came by they came in. But I figured okay, maybe we are on our way somewhere. To the bay, to the bridge, to the shopping center, to a game, to the tree, to the back, somewhere where everyone is, where we will all hang out with a lot of kids, or maybe we are going over to some girls houses, because, yeah I almost forgot about that, this whole thing had changed and anything, anything was possible. But no, it turned out when I got downstairs, onto our front steps, it wasn't the Richie I thought it was, it was a completely different Richie, an older one, the older brother of one of the girls I thought we might go to visit, and he was with this other guy, way older, like 18 or 25. And this older Richie was not friendly and he said, "Where is the fucking money?" I said,

"What money?" He said, "The 800 dollars." I said I didn't have 800 dollars. He said he saw me coming out of his doorway when no one was home. Then the older guy pulled back his jacket just enough so I could see the gun stuck in his belt. And both of them just looked at me like they were gonna kill me. I just stood there shaking my head. I was coming out of his doorway when there was no one home, that part was true. I was with my friends. We were calling for his sister. But she was not home. He said I better get the money back to him by the next day. And they left.

It was hard for me to finish my homework that day. It turned out it was two other kids that stole the money. Richie sold pot. We all knew about it. Richie got the money back later, I heard. Then everything was fine, for me.

When I was 19 my father died. One day his heart stopped beating. He was not old. He didn't smoke. He was trim and played sports. At 53 his heart stopped. It was a gray Monday morning, on a damp street in the Bronx, on the sidewalk in front of his office door. I remembered going there. Hearing the sound of the traffic as if from far away, as if receding, and wondering how everything could just keep going as if nothing had happened.

That year I often listened to my own heartbeat. Whenever I would sit down or lay down, at the end of the day, or in the morning, any time, no matter what else was going on, my mind would drift to the feeling of my own heartbeat. Sometimes I wouldn't notice it, but then I would think, well, I am still alive so it must be beating. It must be okay. Sometimes I would feel it beat. I wondered if that beat would be my last beat. Why would it not be my last one? How would I know? What kept it going? Why would one stop?

3. Dot Head

In karate practice every move you make must be made with intention. You can't just reposition your body in the air, adopt the posture of a punch or a block and think you are really training karate. In karate your intention itself is what you are training.

A kata is a sequence of fighting moves performed against a series of imaginary opponents. It is one of the two primary methods for training in the traditional martial arts—not only on Okinawa, but in China and Japan as well. If kata is trained without intention in the movements it will not be useful for self- defense. If you are training your intention, not just your posture, it is an effective means of perfecting fighting skills.

This is important training for life too, not just for self-defense. Just going through the motions of life with an attitude of fatalism, is appealing to passive people. It's a reflex they can use when the going gets tough: they get to throw up their hands, dismiss their responsibility for their circumstances, say "Life sucks," and get back to aimlessness and self-pity. But if we put our intention into every move of our life, then our life comes to life. And it isn't life happening around us or to us that changes. It is us.

If you teach karate for a while you can see people make this discovery, cross a threshold, and instead of using karate as a hobby or a means to an end they become practitioners.

To make progress we have to go step by step. Or else, intoxicated by the first few exciting steps, we can get into trouble.

There is a point in training, after two or three years, when practitioners begin to feel bold. They feel strong. They lose their fear. I remember when my friends and I were at that stage.

In the '80s, in Purgatory, there was a banker about 30 years old and a very pleasant man. His family came from India and he lived in New Jersey. There, in that part of New Jersey, first-generation Indians were newcomers to the neighborhoods. This American-born Indian man had studied hard and moved away. There were some local boys near the PATH station where the banker got off the train. The banker was wearing a neat blue suit, to visit his parents that afternoon in the summer. A boy and a girl confronted him and said "Go home, dot head." They called all the Indians dot heads. He could have stayed cool. He could have looked at who was talking and considered why and walked away. But he didn't do that. It is hard to do that. Maybe he had been humiliated many times before and now, after a few years of karate training he said to himself: "I deserve respect. I have had enough."

It's hard to stay cool.

He didn't. He decided it was time to stand and fight and not take this bullshit any more. He put his fists up in front of him and glared at the boy and girl. This is not good strategy. A friend of the boy and girl came up behind him silently and crushed his head with a brick. I think if he had had more or less experience in karate he would have walked away or been aware of the danger and defended himself. But he died and we all missed him and were sorry.

It was common at that time in New York to hear stories of encounters with violence from everyone. The streets and subways were dangerous. It was a fact of life in the 1970s and '80s, and the difference between indoors and outdoors was night and day.

4. The Shield

The head of Purgatory, the Boss, was a New York City cop whom I admired. He was 15 years older than I was. He had an authoritative presence.

Police have a clear intention. They are strong. They win. They are the good guys. Intention is attractive. Some teenagers are drawn to the drug world because, at first, it's a focused life. Instead of meaningless drift, TV and anonymity, there is an objective, a hierarchy, and a way to achieve status.

It's why gangs and corporations are appealing. At first joining a group seems like it will make you bigger. It seems to offer a way to extend your self out beyond the boundaries of your own limited life. But the relationship can turn on you. Especially if the mission of the group is greed. Like the mob. Then where are you? Enemies everywhere. Everyone outside is them, everyone inside is us. Everywhere there is a slight, a threat, an attack.

The Boss was our leader, the embodiment of the tough white guy. A street cop with an attitude and a smile.

The way I understood it, there was karate, which was a pure Okinawan cultural artifact, and then, when training was over for the evening and you hung out, there was this other thing. On our own time, this whole other world opened up.

It was a thrill to ride along with the cops, on patrol, at night. There's always something going on. And if there's no action then there is the relentless motor mouth, the gallows humor, the marathon rank-out festival that went on hour after hour after hour. There was no end to the targets. Just drive around.

There's just two kinds of people, they'll tell you, cops and assholes. And look at all the assholes out tonight, look at those scumbags, look at that skel, that mutt, that monkey, hey you want to know what happens from 10 or 15 generations of brother sister fucking, check out this neighborhood....

And these cops are great guys. Love their families. Idealistic, want to do what's right, to protect the citizens from the scumbags. Or want to do their jobs and retire in one piece. They are the good guys. But it seemed, with these guys, that the actual people you actually see on the street are rarely the "citizens" they are sworn to protect. The ones you face on the streets, in the abandoned buildings, in the piss stinking hallways, are the scumbags. That's just the way it is, they say. "If I ain't made sergeant yet, I guess I never will, so I will just do my twenty and get the hell out," one cop said as he drove through darkest Brooklyn. Then: Hey, look at that motherfucker. He's dirty, let's hit him.

And hit him they do. And now it's just some guy with his hands in a flex-cuff, his face against the peeling paint of an old Impala, cursing his luck and saying shit shit shit over and over. And that's the end of the shift. Except on the way back comes a call for a backup on a fire and these guys run into the building, not away from it like any normal person, they run in and get the baby out. Then go home.

And I rode along with them. We all enjoyed that. Even the guy who was driving the cruiser, who, his partner said, had this big ass because he hadn't been out of the cruiser in 18 years, he pulled over a car and went out and checked him for violations. Just to maybe get into the book I might write. You never know. He drove down the hot streets of Brooklyn as we talked. A drunk stumbled into the street right in front of the car. We stopped short. He jumped back so fast it looked like he bounced off the fender. A detective sitting next to me said we should have a bumper sticker that says "Warning, I break for assholes." Or it could say "Warning, I stop at nothing." How about that?

The Boss told me, "There's a million of these cop movies and they mostly are bullshit and every one of those guys on duty tonight as God is my witness had a thousand stories better than anything you would ever see in the movies and Jesus better than that fuckin' Serpico who was in this precinct, in this unit, and was a nothing cop and a total asshole who had more allegiance to the perps than to his own, to the cops." Any one in that car that night had better stories than him. But after a while it seemed that everyone but me wanted to be out there, up there, somewhere, almost anywhere, but here.

And it was just as true for the gangsters, the boys from their hood, guys they grew up with in the old neighborhood in Brooklyn, the guys who went the other way. The cops told me those guys learned how to act from the Godfather. Now these punks are all out there making offers you couldn't refuse, listening to Frank (Sinatra) on the tape player in their Caddies, cruising around the streets of

Brooklyn with a snifter of Chivas balanced on the console, an arm resting on the buttery leather of the seat, draped casually over their girlfriend's thigh....

All was well. Or so it seemed. Peace reigned. I watched. Threats and promises hung in the air over Brooklyn like the sweet smell of the bread baking at the Silvercup Bread factory, at the end of the midnight tour.

5. Okinawa

Creative advertising is designed to disturb your mind. The word creative in this context doesn't mean clever. Some people use it not to describe creating cool concepts and fun images but to the creation of demand. Creating desire where none existed before. Its intention is to disturb you.

The seeds of disturbance exist in our minds. When they are stimulated they cause suffering. The question is what to do about them. Do we knowingly put ourselves into environments where our impulses will be stimulated? Or is it better to create conditions that prevent the seeds of disturbance from germinating?

If we can see that the objects we want cannot satisfy us, but keep us in a perpetual state of want, of disturbance, of dissatisfaction, (suffering), we might decide to stop running after desires.

I wanted to find a Zen teacher when I returned from Okinawa. It was 1988 and I was about to leave my job in advertising to open a karate dojo (training center) somewhere. In preparation for the move I had gone to Okinawa. My objective was to practice karate in a way that I was sure was authentic. I went to see for myself what the Okinawans actually did in their dojos and to see for myself how karate fit in to their lives.

In Okinawa I visited the dojo of Shoshin Nagamine. His framed photograph hung on the front wall of our dojo. I saw it every day and knew his reputation well. The textbook he wrote was our practice bible. An article on Okinawa in National Geographic described him as "the leading figure in Okinawan karate". He was named a "Living National Treasure" by the Japanese government.

In the 1940s and 50s he was chief of police on Okinawa. During the Battle of Okinawa, before the end of World War II, a third of the Okinawan people were killed. They called the battle the "typhoon of steel." Relentless Allied bombardment of the positions of the Japanese Army—dug in, holding Okinawan civilians as human shields, hiding in the limestone caves that snake for hundreds of miles below ground—rained metal and fire on everyone, day after day, for months.

Shoshin Nagamine and everyone he knew had been through hell. All his teachers and many of his friends and family were killed. Some starved. Some had been hostages of the Japanese military. Some were killed by machine gun fire from aircraft as they worked in their fields or walked on the roads.

When the war was over, the traditional agrarian island society was in chaos. There was no economy, no work, no agriculture, almost no food. Just humiliation and pain, and a pervasive sense that life was insane and hope was useless. Unexploded munitions were found in every field, likely to detonate at the touch of a plow blade or a footstep. People came upon them when they were foraging. Children found them when they were playing. Their killing power continued despite the surrender. Young men formed gangs.

Shoshin Nagamine had the idea that their lives could be rebuilt through the practice of karate. People could regain their health and their strength. And regain their dignity, too, despite their loss of freedom under the Japanese Imperial occupation, and now despite the presence of this new, vast, powerful, occupying military force. Karate, he believed, would help rebuild their sense of community and pride in their Okinawan heritage.

He had been practicing karate since he was a boy. In those days karate had been a secret art. The only way to learn it was in private settings, in a garden behind a teacher's house, or at private training halls attended exclusively by the elite. In the 1920s under the aegis of the Japanese military government, a simplified version of karate was introduced into the Okinawan public schools to encourage physical fitness. In Japan this simplified version of karate became Shotokan. Transported to Korea it became tae kwon do. In Okinawa, Shoshin Nagamine opened up a public dojo, and for the first time anyone who wanted formal karate instruction could get it.

Shoshin Nagamine had the vision and the means to offer his people a better life, at a moment when both vision and means were in short supply. He was about 40 years old at that time.

By the time he was in his middle 50s Okinawan society had stabilized. It was still poor, and most of the best land on the island— beautiful beaches and the best farmland—had become American military bases. By then Nagamine's karate was well established on Okinawa. It had also been exported back to the states by some of the thousands of GI's who finished their tours of duty on Okinawa and returned home, and by Okinawan karate practitioners who had emigrated to Hawaii, Argentina and Peru, along with thousands of other Okinawans who left their poor island for better opportunities in the west.

For each difficulty Nagamine faced through the course of his life karate gave him a way to proceed. When he was a young man he wanted to get healthy and strong. As a police officer he needed the toughness, the fighting skills and the reputation that came with proficiency in karate. Moving up through the ranks in the police department it was an advantage to have his officers trained in karate, and training under him. Their group karate practice made them strong and sharp. It inspired their sense of unity. It was a great tool for a leader.

If you are a sincere practitioner, one of the few who does not become complacent, you will have to go deeper than health, strength, toughness, skills, reputation and relationships. At advanced levels of practice there are few road maps that show the way. You have to go it alone. Every sincere practitioner, every mature human being, will reach that point some time.

Seventeenth century Japanese sword master Miyamoto Musashi wrote that it takes a thousand days to forge the spirit and ten thousand days to polish it. Some people interpret that as "a pretty long time" to forge the spirit and "a really long time" to polish it. But I do not think that's what he was saying. 11,000 days. That's thirty years of training along known paths. Then you're on your own.

And Shoshin Nagamine seems to have been aware that he had reached that point when he was 56. In traditional, agrarian societies, where the movements of the stars and planets are noted and significant as current events, people are aware of the importance of this age. Every 56 years the planet Saturn returns to the position in the sky where it was on the day you were born. Some believe that this is an auspicious time or maybe even a last chance to redirect your life toward what will sustain you and help you inwardly be reborn.

During this phase of his life, in the mid 1960s, Shoshin Nagamine sought out Sakiyama Roshi at Kozenji Zendo (Zen practice center and temple) in Shuri Village, for advice and for instruction in Zen meditation. This was the same Sakiyama Roshi who sent me the black belt 30 years later.

Sakiyama Roshi was a man of extraordinary accomplishment. Like Nagamine he had chosen an unusual path through life. He was an Okinawan Zen practitioner for one thing. Okinawan culture and Japanese culture are different, and were often in conflict. Since the Japanese capture of Okinawa in 1879 the Japanese Empire tried by decree and by force, to replace Okinawan culture with Japanese culture. Only Japanese language was taught in the schools. Speaking the indigenous dialect was discouraged.

The practice of Zen was Japanese, not Okinawan. It was closely associated with Japanese military government, as it had been on mainland Japan for centuries. The Okinawan people were not much interested.

The young Sakiyama Sogen was. At the end of World War II, uneducated and penniless, he managed to get off Okinawa by stowing away on a ship. For him it was worth risking everything to study and practice Zen formally in a monastery, face to face with a Zen master. This was not possible on Okinawa. There were no Zen masters there.

Sakiyama Roshi told me about it one evening, at Kozenji. He was in his mid 70s at the time we talked but the adventure, nearly fifty years past, was still fresh in his mind. Eventually he was admitted for training into Enkakuji Temple at Kamakura, where he was ordained by one of the great teachers of the time, Asahina Roshi.

Sakiyama told me: *One encounter can change your whole life. It is essential to encounter one's self. But strangely enough we are ignorant about ourselves and it is not easy to see one's own mind. In order to accomplish this we need to find a master who teaches about life. I couldn't help but do it.*

It was Showa 24—1949, he wrote later. *At that time there was trouble between Okinawa and Japan. I knew it would be difficult. Okinawa was occupied by the U.S. Army and it was illegal to travel between Okinawa and mainland Japan. I sewed $60 into my underwear, to hide it, and arranged to be smuggled out of Okinawa on a small 15 ton fishing boat. I hid with about 20 other people.*

I remember it perfectly, all those people struggling. We were standing way down in the hold of the ship, deep in foul water, for several days. We worked constantly to bail the water out, but it poured in too fast for us. When I close my eyes I can still see it.

When we arrived in Kagoshima we were all arrested and taken to the police station. We were detained. Each day we were interrogated by the prosecutor, asked to explain what we were doing there. It was several weeks before we were released.

*I went to stay with Genchu Yajima at Keizoji Temple in Oita Prefecture.
He welcomed me. I stayed with him for a while. When I left his temple for
Myoshinji monastery in Kyoto he asked each of the parish families who
supported his temple to donate 10 cedar saplings. A little hill sloped up
around the temple gate. Yajima planted these saplings there as a gift for my
departure for Myoshinji monastery.*

*He said 'I will look forward to seeing which matures first: you or
these trees.' Five years later I heard he passed away. I felt so clearly that
no matter how wonderful our encounters with people may be, the sense of
impermanence is always present.*

*When I visited his grave at his temple years later I saw the cedar trees he
planted towering above me, shooting way up into the sky. I was so moved by
this as I remembered my late teacher.*

*I was staying in Kyoto at that time. The cold climate there chilled me
to the marrow. I felt assaulted by the cold, attacked by the severity of the
practice there. I made lots of mistakes. Sometimes I was so overwrought
and frustrated I would sneak away to a corner of the garden and cry. Still, I
stayed there two years.*

*I heard about (the great Zen Master) Gempo Yamamoto. I went to
Ryutakuji temple in Izumishima where he was the teacher. I saw this 80-
year old Roshi still radiating dignity. I felt that I had found a place where I
could practice zazen—seated meditation—as I wanted to.*

*Gempo Roshi often said: 'Practice with spirit so strong you can take out
the eyes of a flying horse.' These words encouraged me as a young monk.*

Seven years later Gempo Roshi left this world, closing his eyes on his 95 years of life.

After the funeral ceremony I left for Izu, where I stayed for many years. I went to Enkakuji temple in Kamakura, led by Sogen Asahina Roshi. He was a man of faith, continually praying for the world.

The further you go in practice, the more you discover there is to explore. Asahina Roshi often hit his disciples very hard, painfully. He was never stingy about it. But there was never a single thought of calculation in it. His whole body and mind were filled with a passion to make something out of his disciples.

He radiated intense energy. One day, after we finished with an important conversation inside Roshi's room, I bowed, preparing to leave. At the moment when I raised my head suddenly he hit me. I thought my eardrum was broken. At that moment a second blow came. I couldn't understand what happened. My mind went blank.

This was the first time I could really call Asahina Roshi my father from the bottom of my heart. I deeply felt the respect, intimacy and trust implied in the word 'father.' Roshi, who raised me, departed for the eternal journey less than a month later. It is impossible for me to express my feelings of gratitude toward my late Roshi.

It was hard for me to understand this. It sounds sadistic. But if we understand the connection between the trainee and the teacher, the motivation of the teacher, the skill in choosing the perfect moment of the strike—and the profound, transformative result that came from it, we can begin to see. We should not yield too soon to our prejudices when we hear stories like this.

As a young monk, long ago in post-war Japan, Sogen Sakiyama trained vigorously. He told me that very often he and his closest friend, Tai Shimano now Eido Roshi, head of Dai Bosatsu Monastery in Livingston Manor, New York, would sit face to face in seated meditation all night. These two young men were fanatical in their dedication to training and they encouraged each other.

As they both have described it to me they sat on their meditation cushions in full lotus position. Across their knees each had a keisaku. A keisaku is a flat 'encouragement stick' used in some Japanese Zen temples by senior monks who make the rounds, walking up and down behind the rows of monks sitting in meditation. When they see that one is dozing or lax in practice the senior will stop behind him, turn toward him, bow and then strike him sharply on the shoulder muscles. The strikes sharpen the monk's attention, and the thwack! thwack! echoing through the silent meditation hall sharpens everyone else's too.

Sakiyama and Eido would sit on into the night, face to face. When one would nod off the other would wake him up with a whack of the keisaku across the shoulder, and the two would continue to meditate till dawn.

Years later Sakiyama was confirmed as a Roshi, a Zen Master, having completed his study. Soon afterwards he was installed as abbot of Kozenji Zen temple in his home prefecture of Okinawa. Kozenji is a small temple, beautifully built in traditional style, with meticulously polished hardwood floors, white walled interiors, as spare as a Shaker sitting room, graceful as a willow. It sits on top of the highest hill on Okinawa, next to Shuri Castle, the seat of the Okinawan monarchy for more than 500 years. Shuri Castle was bombed during the war. Recently it has been rebuilt as a museum and park. When Shoshin Nagamine went to visit Kozenji in the early 1960s, only the castle gate and the crumbling ruined stone walls remained.

What did this place mean to Shoshin Nagamine? Was it a reminder of impermanence? Of mutability? Of mortality? Of the end of Okinawan identity? Or had he seen so much destruction already, it made no special impression at all?

Shoshin Nagamine, karate master and Chief of Police, studied Zen with Sakiyama Roshi. Sakiyama had been a karate practitioner for many years. The two men understood each other. Nagamine frequently meditated at Kozenji Zendo. He encouraged his students to meditate, and began a Zen meditation group at his dojo in Naha, a few miles away.

Dokusan is the name for the formal face-to-face interviews that take place at regular intervals between a Zen master and a student. It is an essential part of Rinzai style Zen practice. Traditionally this is the setting in which the Zen student presents his understanding to his teacher. In response to the student's presentation the Zen teacher will either confirm his insight or else, much more commonly, send him back to the meditation hall for more practice.

Dokusan, Sakiyama Roshi said to me, must be "Real combat
with real swords." The body and mind must be that alert. And the
stakes are that high. There are some Zen teachers who use the sword
metaphor as hyperbole. He did not.

Shoshin Nagamine did dokusan with Sakiyama Roshi.

When I met Nagamine he was in his 80s. His back was bent, he
moved his feet gingerly when he walked and he had a difficult time
seeing. The training at his dojo was led by his senior students, men
in their 50s and 60s. He took everyone by surprise one evening when
I was training at his dojo when he put on a gi and taught.

Later on that night we talked for quite a while.

One morning a few days later, I took a walk through the streets
of Naha, Okinawa's capital city. I wandered along the Kokusai Dori,
International Avenue, enjoying the cool morning air. The island is
only a few miles wide, so the scent of the ocean is everywhere. The
roofs in that section of town were in traditional style, curved red
terra cotta tile. Almost all the houses had a pair of chisa, lion dogs,
perched on top, keeping a lookout for evil spirits.

The sun was coming up. I wandered down the back streets
toward the Nagamine dojo. The entry is up a few steps leading onto
a low loading dock. The family-run grocery store next door wasn't
open yet. But in the shadows, protected from the brilliant daylight
outside, I saw some people seated. Appearing in the doorway,
standing just a few feet away, Shoshin Nagamine recognized me. He
came to the edge of the doorway, just into the warm daylight. He

gestured for me to come in. I did. He gestured to me to take a seat
on one of the dozen round black cushions placed in rows on the
floor. Most of the cushions were occupied. Men, mostly in business
clothes, were sitting cross-legged on them. I sat down. While all the
other people seemed content and comfortable, I struggled not to
tip over. My legs were thick and stiff. A bell rang three times from
somewhere off behind me. The stillness got deeper as the meditation
period began.

I spoke very little Japanese. So even if I had time to ask a
question about what to do while I was sitting there, or how long I
would be sitting there, it is unlikely that I would have understood. I
just sat there as happy as can be. Thinking, this is so cool. The real
thing. Great. Then another thought crowded across my mind: This is
really, really painful.

Within minutes I was sitting in a pool of pure pain, wishing one of these guys would stand up and, well they looked like samurais, so maybe one would kindly chop my head off and put an end to it. Nevertheless I refused to move. I quivered, trembled, shook, sweated and prayed but I didn't move till the bell sounded and all the other people stood up and bowed to the altar and bowed to each other and went off to work.

I wanted to train deeply. I looked for a place to learn about Zen when I came back home.

6. Many Mansions

I searched around for a place to practice where I would feel
as at home as I had on Okinawa. I ardently checked things out. I
had done this kind of searching before. Years before I searched for
churches. Sunday mornings and weekday evenings.

I went to a grand and gloomy Gothic cathedral way uptown.
Stained glass and stone and history and beauty, all belonged to
someone else and to another world. A world of statues, peacocks,
private meetings where we discussed Celts and giant vegetables
and the dawning of the Age of Aquarius. To the knave, the clouds
swirling and the censors swinging, came the processionals and the
calls to put an end to war. To the world went Cumbayah, tracts,
sincerity and good works.

The neighborhood church on the Lower East Side, always full, a
spiritual home and a feeling of home for immigrants newly arrived
from the Ukraine.

The hip church where everyone kept hugging each other during
the services and anyone could receive sacraments, no questions asked.

Services in storefronts. Six rows of metal folding chairs, listeners
waiting for coffee, enjoying a respite from the cold world, a moment
of peace, a prayer.

At a service in a concert hall the stage was decked with flowers
and organ music and pamphlets in gold italic type on thin delicate
paper. We felt the enthusiasm of the grandfatherly minister on stage,

his voice rising and falling in regular waves, exultation and warning, admonishing us to follow the Example and gain the Splendor, or endure the Wrath.

At a holy rollin' revival in a big hall on the outskirts of a suburban town the bass guitar boomed, the band rocked and a three screen slide show flooded the stage with light and images of the life, death and resurrection, backlighting the perspiring minister in a halo of blazing gold, amber and blue… his amplified voice carrying the gospel beyond the cinderblock walls, echoing in our chests, as if the power of the sound itself could fill the Jesus shaped hole in our hearts.

A small hall of Anthroposophists. A dozen faithful on a sunny Sunday on the Upper West Side, praying, reflecting, attending to the lecturers.

Everywhere I went people were sincerely seeking and were finding… something. I believed that I would find something too. I believed that it would be outside me, that I would encounter it and learn it and understand it and then what was missing would be found. So I kept going.

I heard about love. Mercy. Grace… Wonderful.

But the means? How would I experience these when the world seemed so thoroughly arranged to provide the opposite? By changing my own mind? By adjusting my own way of life? I never thought of that.

We tend to believe the ideas we learn as children. Then we test our experiences against these first-formulations, and assign our experiences meaning within a framework of these ideas. We also tend to select for experiences that confirm our ideas. These early ideas, our organizing principles, gradually structure our minds. They then cease to be identifiable to us as ideas in the mind.

My early organizing principles failed to provide either predictive ability or happiness. Some of the organizing principles that I tested along the way were:

1. An unseen power will reward you when you are good and punish you when you are bad.

2. It is impossible to understand what I going on.

3. Life is random. Events are meaningless.

4. The universe is mechanical. Events are foreordained.

5. Virtuous action causes happiness and non-virtuous action brings suffering—by the very nature of reality and of our own minds.

Most of us may rely on one of these more than the others, perhaps picking up one when it is convenient, and switching to another when that seems to provide a more satisfying explanation or plan. After a while we can see that, if followed consistently, each one will produce a different kind of life.

7. Sherlock's Craft

Everyone likes stories. "Once upon a time" lands softly on your ears and you sit back and listen. Sitting around a campfire, a hearth, in a cave, in a tent, in an igloo, in an arena, a theater, a living room, a dinner table, everyone likes a story. Why is that?

In transcendental meditation they say that thoughts 'bubble up' in your mind. Uchiyama Roshi, a great modern Zen master, says the mind naturally 'secretes' thought. They recommend different ways of dealing with thought but they both use metaphors to explain that the mind naturally tends to move.

We enter the world wanting. We look for ways to get what we want. Soon after we get what we want we want something else. What is consistent is the mental condition of wanting. We are always in that condition. When we are satisfied we begin to crave desire. Stories are about wanting. Every story has a person who wants something and takes action to get what he wants. He attains it or doesn't attain it.

Stories end arbitrarily. That is (unlike the non-subjective infinite flow of life in time, space and mind) stories reach a certain point and cut off. It may feel satisfying or unsatisfying to the listener, but at some point they just stop. If the objective established at the outset of the story is getting the girl, lets say, then the story may end with a marriage. If it's a homecoming story maybe they live happily ever after. Those are arbitrary endings. Marriage, in life, may end one set of wants but it doesn't end wanting.

Stories work because we sense that there is an imbalance of energy—a lack or an excess—and out there somewhere there's something that will satisfy the desire and create a harmonious condition. Resolving the imbalance is the goal of the story. It is called a resolution. When Sherlock Holmes has a rainy afternoon to putter around his flat he is disturbed by a knock on the door. The feeling, unstated, but palpable, is that while he may seem irritated by the knock that disturbs his puttering-in-peace in fact he is relieved by the knock on the door because the static coziness of the flat is producing an undercurrent of anxiety in his mind: he knows this peace will soon become boring.

It is the knowing that he will be disturbed by a knock on the door that allows us—that makes us—savor the Lamarckian orderliness of Sherlock's empire. The rest of the Sherlock Holmes story comes from Sherlock's efforts to solve the case. The action of the story is driven forward by his skillful efforts to restore the order that has been disturbed: to get back to his cozy flat and his classifying of the lepidoptera, or tobacco ash samples or whatever he was doing when the story began. The state of resolution, when attained, contains the fast blooming seed of boredom, which spurs us readers on to the next tale and the next: disturbed and satisfied, again and again and again.

And so it is with our pursuit of food, sex, sleep, money and status. Like the structure of our mind itself. Endlessly shifting, endlessly striving toward resolution, disturbed again as the seed of boredom blooms. What is the source of the boredom? The long-ingrained mental habit of wanting. Is this propensity built into the structure of the brain? Is it psychological habit?

Is it inevitable?

Zen Master Uchiyama Roshi often talks about the significance
of the experience of boredom in long Zen meditation retreats.
Boredom is a highly unappealing, unromantic aspect of spiritual
practice. It is not the kind of thing nice sincere spiritual people
discuss. It is not inspiring, like the heroism of dedicating your life
to saving all beings as expressed in say, the writing of the ancient
Indian Buddhist master Shantideva. Shantideva is inspiring. He uses
the story structure to set us on the path to Buddhahood.

Uchiyama Roshi's presentation is quite different. He just sits
down on the cushion and there he is. He dares you to have the
courage to just face the wall. For five days, or ten days, cross-
legged, immobile, 14 hours a day, silent, facing the blank wall. No
one can do that on will power or discipline alone. In Uchiyama
Roshi's approach to Zen meditation, called Just Sitting, something
astonishing is going on. We hardly have a precedent for it in our
experience. There's no story there. It did not sound too promising to
me as the key to freedom when I first heard about it.

8. Door Number One

I looked in the phone book for Zen and even in the largest city in the country there were only two listings. I called and got no answer. Nowadays that is almost unimaginable but in those days, even after everyone had read D.T. Suzuki, Alan Watts, Alan Ginsberg, Jack Kerouac, William Burroughs, Gary Snyder, page after page in praise of Zen, it was still hard to actually find in America east of California.

I went to the door of an apartment whose address was listed in the phone book under Zen and knocked on a door and a sleepy guy in a bathrobe came to the door and rubbed his face and told me to go away! But... I was on the path! I was ready to be enlightened! And this guy knew Zen and he didn't care, he just told me to go away. Hmmm, I said to myself, Zen is not what I thought!

Now, when people pop in on me unexpectedly at the door of my dojo, and I ask them to come back at the scheduled time for meditation practice, and they look at me disappointed, surprised that I don't stop what I am doing and offer them some tea and join them in an experience like the one they imagined that they would have, I know how they feel. I usually invite them to come back later, when the Zen group meets.

But back then, in the 70s, I prowled the shelves at Weiser's bookstore on Broadway near Saint Mark's, looking. Slipping in and out among the aisles filled with ...who were those people? Were they witches? Tarot readers, astrologers, swamis, yogis, ascended masters, secret sharers, fellow travelers, snake handlers, vegetarians, students from NYU? I had no way to distinguish between them as I tried to find some guidance about spiritual things, but no, no matter how much I read I could not find much at all.

So naturally when I saw the ad in a magazine for a Zen meditation center I arranged a visit.

9. The Human Realm

In the dark in a hurry in the midst of what was to me the magnificent great north woods, the bus wound its way around the last bend in the road, and at the end of a little bridge it stopped and wheezed and I got off. I breathed the fresh air and slung my little bundle over my shoulder. It bounced against my thigh as I walked up the driveway between the tall tall pines past the gray sea dragon and into the heavy thick dark wooden doorway.

Hello.

I joined in the sitting meditation, cross-legged on a cushion on the floor. It hurt my legs. I was a beginner. I listened to the lectures. I didn't follow what they were saying. This was the way it was supposed to be, I guessed. I slept on my bunk. I was bored and tired. I missed karate practice. This visit was only for a few days. But for the previous ten years I had practiced karate every day. For the last five years I had practiced four or five hours every day. Now I missed it.

Each day for years I trained karate. First on the roof of my building for an hour in the morning, then at a noon workout at the dojo in midtown, and then an evening workout following work on the weekdays, or on my roof again on the weekends. Now I was sitting still.

This place up here in the woods a few hours north of the city, didn't seem very much like what I envisioned a Zen place to be. In my imagination it was, first of all, supposed to be either China—on top of a steep mountain in a sea of pointed mountains fading off into the misty distance—or Japan, in black and white. This was like summer camp.

When you are new and enthusiastic you think you've got it. You pick up a few basic techniques, some procedures, vocabularies, customs, and pretty soon it seems a whole new, more sensible world is opening up to you. As you proceed, going deeper, as your new hobby, religion, profession or sport becomes a practice, something integrated into the way you are living, day in and day out, you will encounter difficulties. There is a strong temptation at that point to back off. It takes a combination of enthusiasm, faith in the efficacy of practice and an experienced teacher, to get through the obstacles and attain a higher level of skill.

An experienced teacher will put beginners under pressure. Make demands on them that the beginners must meet and that, as a result, will change them in a healthful way. Immature or insecure people will put up with hazing, condescension, all sorts of negative emotional states, in order to be accepted, even into an unhealthy group. Their need to be a member will supersede all their other agendas. That is how cults work. It is not how a good dojo or a good meditation group works.

Now I am a teacher. Then I was a beginner. Now I know that in modern life, with so many choices so many distractions and temptations, every person who comes sincerely looking for help has to be taken seriously. Despite whatever weaknesses or misunderstandings they may have you have to show them a way to go forward. It's hard for teachers to do this consistently because most of these needy newcomers don't last long. You give your energy and they quit anyway. It is taxing. But it's your job.

At that Zen center there were teachers not ready to teach. They had the shaved heads and the robes and the form of practice, but not the heart of it.

In medieval Japan institutional Zen was a state-supported church and a career choice as well as a possible spiritual path. Temples and monasteries offered newcomers a total immersion environment in which they could be supported while they learned and grew and trained and reached maturity as practitioners and as human beings. Under the guidance of sincere, generous and accomplished masters, with the reputation and the toughness required, profound transformation would arise in willing students. That was the ideal. Sometimes it was realized.

Feudal craft guilds worked in a similar way. Newcomers began with little or no formal education, and significantly, with few alternatives. You did what you were told, you learned, you were supported, you worked hard, you were promoted, if you demonstrated the ability you might have the opportunity to lead, to teach, and perhaps to achieve mastery. Within each guild there were a few elite individuals and many who supported them. There were many others who humbly and simply worked their trade for a living. It was a matter of power, reinforced by social mythology, and a fact of life.

Modern people acting out their fantasy of what medieval Japanese people did is not 'keeping the tradition pure.' It is turning a living tradition to stone. And over the years groups of

underdeveloped and overly ambitious American Zen practitioners
have based their claims to legitimacy on the approval of the
Japanese Zen institution. But these same Americans do not accept
the guidance or authority of their Japanese teachers, and when the
Japanese have criticized their approach these Americans walk out of
the meetings in a huff.

Could it be a matter of self-deception manifest in slick marketing
that worked for a while when Buddhism first came to America, at a
time when few westerners had the experience to distinguish between
genuine spiritual teaching and a charismatic individual with real
estate, a special outfit and haircut?

To teach effectively you have to talk to people, explain why,
guide them with understanding and friendship, with high demands
and expectations, scrupulously apply pressure that they willingly
take on, which they understand to be in their interest to bear. If you
properly, incrementally, increase the level of challenge over time,
success can come. Without that careful consideration of what their
students need day to day, teachers just inculcate affectations in their
students. And the idealistic young students turn into discouraged,
middle aged people wondering if this is all there is to spiritual life.

The Zen training I encountered on Okinawa was rigorous
and unpretentious. The Zen training I found at that center was
concerned with persuading people—of the superiority of that style,
of the need to spend a lot of money on their programs, of the need
to place your affiliation with them above all else in your life. It
seemed to me the opposite of spiritual life.

Neediness on the part of leaders cannot help people be strong, or healthy, or mature. These unprepared leaders cannot help forge in the hearts of their students a refuge from suffering.

And yet... when the place was silent, I was moved by something I felt present there. It was there whether the great hall was empty or full. Empty it was a vast cavern of shadows and infinite possibility. Full, with a hundred people sitting silently, the space above them shimmering with peace: how extraordinary, how rare to see people like this.

The somber intonation of the bells. Reminding. Alerting. Sounding like they echoed from the depth of space and time. The solemn clap clap! of the woodblock, the steady rhythm of the wooden fish struck in time to the chanting, pressing in against my ears and out against the walls. There was some feeling, a memory or a yearning, a longing, a feeling of time passing, of one more page turned, one more day lived, one more chance to realize the truth and be free, a moment, come and gone....

And so my disappointment was so much deeper when I found myself unable to reconcile that deep experience of the form of practice and the form of worship as it evaporated into the ordinary clubbiness of that culture, and their defensive claim that their way as the only pure, true and legitimate way. How could these same people —nice, nervous, confident, pretentious, sincere, foolish, whatever— be the ones who created that marvel I witnessed and I participated a few minutes before?

I did not understand the efficacy of well-created form: how to sit, how to stand, how to walk, how to eat, how to sleep, how to chant… I could not appreciate what was available. The form was created by generations of geniuses. The form seeps in as you practice, and as it does your inner life changes. As it does your mind and body change to fill the form more and more completely, more accurately, more naturally.

It's easy to see, now, because I have gone through it, in the karate dojo and in the Zendo (meditation hall.) Now I have known thousands of people who have undertaken it.

Transformation by following the form works in the practice of kata —the formal movement sequences of karate—and it works in the practice of zazen—seated meditation. First you imitate the form. Then you fill it with life.

It works, and it doesn't take long. It has a perceptible effect on the people practicing, even if they are new at it, even if their accomplishment is not yet deep and their mind and motivation are far from matching the potential offered by the form. Still they experience results from practice. Even if a moment after they stand, or after they finish their kata, the nobility of their practice persona instantly dissolves and their awkward, rough-edged, ordinary self re-emerges. Watch a child finish a kata with amazing focus and self-possession and then, an instant after completing the moves, bowing and then running around, jumping and giggling. The practitioner aura dissolves but the evidence of the practice is real.

Form can be superficially embodied or deeply embodied. It won't transform the practitioner permanently any more than one session of weight lifting would turn the weekend wannabe into a Navy SEAL. But wholeheartedly living out enlightened form, over time, has a profound transformative result.

As I began my practice life, my habits of mind, were mixed, not pure. The good part—the results of my previous virtuous actions—allowed me to be moved by the profound feeling of the form of practice. But that strong connection was overwhelmed time and again by my hasty judgments of others. What I was unable to see, what was blocked by my own small-mindedness was: which should I judge to be more important? Which should I ignore, and which might offer something of enormous value to me?

10. Pen & Sword

I had gone through a similar experience when looking for a martial arts place years before. I felt the same hope, excitement and disappointment, and exercised the same persistence, too. I knew there was something out there that would match what I imagined, however vaguely I imagined it. There was a way I wanted to feel and a way I wanted to live and I was determined to find it. I had some idea from the TV show Kung Fu.

I met someone in college who practiced a martial art. He was a few years older than I was. He was a strong, tough looking guy. I was an editor of the school paper and he wrote a piece for it. It was an article about a strike at a factory, about city politics and the unions. It wasn't the kind of piece we usually ran, but he said he wanted to do it and he dug into the subject and found the people and got the interviews and put the story together. It was the kind of story that if you presented yourself as a student reporter for the university newspaper they would tell you to buzz off. But he wouldn't buzz off. He had a confidence and swagger to him, and he made it work. You don't see that in every writer. Okay, martial arts then.

11. The Investigation

I looked for places to practice martial arts in various towns where I lived and I felt in each one a disappointment: mostly that they were taking themselves too seriously and their practice not seriously enough. After all there is no real hope of a payoff in the martial arts other than the benefits of practice itself. There is no possibility of money or fame, power or status, on any scale bigger than your own club. But still, people seek those things from it.

That is a crossroads martial arts practitioners reach at some time in their careers. Take one road, you mature. You take on the pressures and the challenges and the obstacles, inside and out, and you get strong and humble and clear about what you are up to.

Take the other road you become a phony, a big frog in a little pond, a tin soldier. Sometimes people who start out sincerely get confused when they've had a small taste of status and strength.

Status matters to us. If someone feels frustrated with their social status or their profession or how much money they make, they may turn to something else in the hopes of elevating their status—in their own eyes and the eyes of others. If they try to do this in martial arts they will get frustrated, and may begin trying to impress people with their ranks, titles, secret knowledge, or importance in some imaginary world. It is silly. Status seeking for its own sake, when it is not earned by genuine effort and mastery, looks foolish. Since status is so important to people, people who try to fake it are easily detected and shunned.

But people who are humble and honest and work hard can succeed. Parents who lose their relationship with their teenaged children are ones who are perceived by the teenagers as being either losers or phonies. The parents who are honest and direct have better relationships with their teenage children. Especially when we are young we are attracted to status and repelled by hypocrisy. These values informed my search for a place to practice and for people to emulate.

Over five years in the late 70s and early 80s I checked out many places, of many different styles. I joined half a dozen during that period and practiced in some for several years. There was variation in the details but each time the pattern was the same. I read the literature. I talked to the teacher. I watched a class. Enthusiastic, I joined. I got the uniform. I learned the procedures. I practiced the basics. I talked to the other beginners. I threw myself into practice. Each time I felt disappointed: in the place, the style, the teacher, myself, or some combination of them all.

Soft sunlight slid through the shades, across the hard polished wood floor of the tai chi studio. Three flights of steps above a loading dock, just off Sixth Avenue. The room was silent. I was bursting with energy. My chest and arms were big from a few years of weight lifting at my college wrestling team's weight room. I was running a few miles a day, and I never, ever missed training. I joined in with the tai chi routine. It was slow. Now everyone knows tai chi is slow but then I didn't know it at all. There were dancers there, an air of California about the place. I sweated. The teacher told me not to sweat. I liked to sweat. Too much chi, he told me. Forget that.

I practiced tae kwon do. I got my fingers jammed while sparring on the first day, but that did not stop me. I figured it was my fault. Loose fist. In a matter of weeks the swelling went down, and I kept going. We did muscle ripping ballistic stretches in the air, and tendon tearing two-man stretches at the wall. We bounced and bobbed and kicked over our heads. We got sore, we swore, we tore into our workouts like we were on fire, for 90 seconds at a time. Then we talked a little, admired someone's technique, or commented on how this person was good, this person would never be good, this person was incredible and would definitely be someone who would go really far, someone we would be hearing a lot about in the years to come.

There were two false propositions that I subscribed to in that setting. 1. That there was a heap, and 2. I ought to be on top of it.

It turns out there isn't a heap. There were hundreds of little heaps —hundreds of tournaments and thousands of clubs—and there was no top to any of them. The personnel were always changing, the injury rate was high, careers were short, you were a good athlete or you weren't when you walked in the door, but only a little seemed to change as a result of training.

It is great to feel that push, that rush, that fear and that challenge every time you go out there to spar. It is thrilling, and it puts urgency in your training. For a season, a year or two. But it doesn't stay. And then you retire (i.e. quit), or you pay for it with injuries and a feeling of lost possibility that, for many people, never goes away.

And lots of the martial arts people I met cultivated a mental attitude that seemed silly. Strutting and puffed up. Who is impressed by this? This is not medieval Japan where samurais rule the roads, and being a trained martial artist gave you status and power. We are not gangsters. We modern guys were getting stronger and faster and more flexible from training. But why act puffed up about it? You want power become a Senator. You want status, try Wall Street. Want to preen and be admired for your handsomeness and wonderfulness? Try show business. But to achieve those ends through the martial arts? You'll be disappointed.

Who needs that, I thought to myself? What happened to inner peace and everything? What happened to Keith Carridine and his very old Kung Fu teacher?

I tried aikido. It was fun for me. But? I did not believe that it was morally superior to drop someone on their head and break their neck than to punch them in the nose if they were attacking you. In fact I thought the latter seemed a better choice for everyone. And I was not convinced by the idea that using the opponent's force against him or moving in a circular fashion was unique to aikido. All martial arts do that. The attacks seemed too soft to really test anything but a willingness to cooperate. Surely I judged too hastily.

I loved the atmosphere. The Japanese style was thrilling. The artifacts, the shrine and the calligraphy. The simple functionality of the room. The bowing and the one right way to do everything. But I couldn't get a workout.

Now, more than twenty years later, I use many of the same techniques, interpretations and practice methods used in tai chi and aikido every day. These are common to karate and many martial arts, and the insights gleaned from those Chinese and Japanese traditions bring many once obscure aspects of karate kata vividly to life. But when I first encountered them these martial arts were lacking something that I wanted, but which I could not define.

The kind of workout I was looking for was what I got in the mountains. On my vacations from college I traveled up to the White Mountains in New Hampshire, usually alone. I would walk for a week or two. I would walk all day, 10 or 12 hours, every day, fast, keeping my body hot so I could go in a T-shirt in weather that was freezing.

Steam poured off my body when I stopped for a drink. The water tasted pure and the scent of the evergreen trees clinging to the rocky ground for life filled my lungs with what my lungs were made to be filled with. The vistas from a mile up leapt into my eyes and I could do anything. Confinement, gravity and the limitations of my body and mind, relationships, biography and destiny, became blessedly irrelevant.

I wanted to get that feeling from martial arts practice too.

Sometimes people ask which martial art is best? Before I answer I suggest they first figure out what makes a great life. Then they can choose a style and use it to make their life the life they want. There was no one to tell me that when I was first searching around. And I doubt I could have understood it.

12. Our Lord

I turned to martial arts for two reasons. One, martial arts had to do with Buddhism. To me Buddhism was complete. I believed it could answer any question, solve any difficulty. It had something to do with a personal experience of enlightenment, the highest possible goal a person could have. I figured it ought to be my goal.

There was a second reason. Fighting was a part of life. I encountered it frequently. I didn't like it but if it came up I wanted the advantage. I wanted to protect decent people from thugs. Fights broke out at school and in my neighborhood, every day. From what I'd heard, it happened all over the world and throughout history. It was not okay with me.

I felt that it was the responsibility of each decent person to get the power necessary to defeat predators. What was I supposed to do? Accept that if some jerk came along with a malicious attitude that I was out of luck? Forget it. I never wanted to feel the fear again I felt as a kid growing up when I was hanging out in the school yard with a bunch of friends and the hitters came over the hill, came inside the chain-link fenced-in asphalt playground we all used to play in very nicely and started swinging big garrison belts at our heads making a lot of my friends bleed from their heads and others run away. That was how it went the first time.

The second time that the hitters came to the schoolyard, a few weeks later, we went nuts. We went completely wild, and it was two of their guys that went to the hospital that time. It was better.

Or when this or that older kid would provoke a fight with me or someone else on the bus in junior high or high school. If you tried to walk away they would follow you. Or if you got to their stop and they had to get off before you there they would be the next day, threatening you before school, busting your balls during lunch, smacking you in the back of the head while you were not looking, facing off with you at the bus stop, till finally you hauled off and smacked them across the face. Or they cracked you. Then you could be friends. Of course some guys seemed to breeze through. That made an impression on me that stuck.

There was the time when I was cornered in a handball court, in a part of the schoolyard far from the teachers. Three kids came up close to me. They were angry. They stared at me. They said: "You killed our lord!"

Their leader paused for a moment, to let the power of this accusation sink in, holding back, unable to wait another minute before he did something to redress the wrong he had discovered. "You killed our goddam lord." He said it as if he recognized me from somewhere else.

I had no idea what he was talking about. None. It flashed through my mind that they were thinking of someone else, some other kid maybe that they took me for, because I knew for sure I didn't kill anybody. I certainly didn't kill anyone's lord. I didn't know anyone who had a lord. I thought it was strange that they had a lord, but that maybe they lived under feudalism in their neighborhood. I really thought that might be it. But they were moving closer to me, and threatening me, so I punched one in the face and ran away. It did not feel like a satisfying solution. It was confusing to me: I didn't know what started the problem, and I didn't know if it was over. But it was. They never spoke to me after that.

So what an appealing combination, in a David Carridine sort of way: Buddhism and martial arts.

13. Debbie's Boast

Across the street from my High School was a park, one block square, which before and after school and during lunch periods, filled up with kids. Bunches of kids clung close together and talked about getting into concerts at the Filmore by slipping through the manhole cover in the middle of Second Avenue, right under the feet of the crowds and the cops. We talked about what the Grateful Dead song Uncle John's Band was really about, about Jackson Brown and how Bob Dylan's backup band, The Band, made their own album and it would totally change your life. People asked who had the calculus homework and who was ready for the bio test, and we all really hoped there would be another moratorium so we could protest the war and they would cancel school again for a few days because really everyone had strong feelings about that and we ought to express them. I mean it was our right according to the Constitution, we all agreed, and Thomas Jefferson himself said there ought to be a revolution every 20 years, so the teachers and the administration and the government and all that should be happy really that they are just getting away with a protest and a moratorium because we feel very strongly about this and we are not children, we are 15. We all were and especially I was, on the lookout for that girl that I just talked to that, just for some reason I could never explain, and that no one would understand any way, I had been thinking about and thinking about all day and all night, and you can't get her face and her unbelievable body out of your tormented mind when all you really want to do is see her, but if you don't finish studying chapter seven (The Cell) of the bio book (How Life Works) and memorize the parts of the cell and the parts of the parts of the cell and how they all work (in harmony like a machine, like an orchestra...) like a rock band!, that's it! the teacher said, he was a guy, a young guy, staying out of the war by teaching us, he grew his hair long, he let his freak flag fly, he knew all about San Francisco, he said he planned to go there he said he would live on Van Nuys Street and go to Haight Ashbury and it would be incredible, yes it would be groovy, and yet and yet if I didn't memorize that chapter then no matter how cool he was, my future and nearly as important my weekend, was over. So I was thinking about that while I was walking down the street with one arm carrying my books and the other arm draped around Debbie, my girlfriend.

My arm was wrapped so far around Debbie that my armpit was behind her neck, snug as a life preserver. I leaned upon her like she was a crutch, as if I would fall over without her little five foot self to hold me up. This lean was a declaration of our love. Maybe it was the time of life or maybe the time of man, but it was accepted, embraced really, by us all. This was the way we walked. Together, as one. We are going out, it announced. We were happy.

A car was parked on the wide, busy street between the park and the school. An aging Chevy. There were four guys in it. The windows were open, elbows were hanging out. They were having their last cigarette before the long hard day of school began. I knew one of these guys from shop. Which I hated, mainly because I kept screwing up my wood, and I was not allowed to get a new piece, which seemed unreasonable. The whole shop thing seemed unreasonable. But this guy did fine there. One of the other guys was one of the "goddam lord" guys from the schoolyard that time a few years before. They still used hair tonic to comb their hair. They were wearing short black leather jackets a little longer than baseball jackets, cabrettas, cut square, at the bottom.

Debbie looked in the windows and the guys looked back and I guess she must have read a little attitude in their faces because Debbie said: "My boyfriend can kick your ass." Oh shit, Deb.

I had a situation that demanded the utmost suavity. I was not that suave. But I knew that whether I confirmed or denied or took no position, I was screwed. So I did what I had to do. I looked at Debbie, not with worry, just a little perturbed, a tad disapproving, miffed, and then I looked at the guys, and shook my head as if to say "women." Hey, guys, come one, we're all 15, we know the score. That was that. Or maybe they didn't hear what she said. Anyway, I appreciated her confidence in me. I was sure that, properly handled and in the fullness of time, inspiring that much confidence in others, especially women, could be good.

14. Ten Years of Sweat

I was in my mid-twenties when my martial arts training began for real, and the next ten years were soaked in sweat. I trained every day, everywhere I went. And I went to a lot of places. I trained in the mountains and on the beach.

One time just after dawn a cop came roaring over the dunes in his jeep. He pulled up a few yards away and slowly got out and walked over, raised his hand with a small wave hello, and asked me what I was doing. I thought I was under arrest until he took off his aviator shades and told me that he recognized one of the kata I was doing from his own style but didn't recognize the rest of the kata I was doing, and he wanted to know all about my lineage and where

I learned and who I trained with and if I knew his teacher and if I would like to stop by and attend a class at his dojo nearby that night.

I trained in the Palm Court at the Beverly Hills Hotel. I went down there at 4 a.m. because as far as I could tell as I wandered around looking for a place to train it was the only uninhabited flat spot in the hotel that was big enough for a workout unobserved. I had all the wrong feelings for the Beverly Hills Hotel. It is too fancy for me, but good for the people I was working for, people who's perquisites included not only suites at the best hotels in whatever cities we were visiting but keeping their staff happy and handy at all times. So there I was. But I was so intoxicated by training, by making sure my regimen was fully executed, the string of days of training unbroken, I was oblivious to the delights of the place, and completely unaware of the coolness of it. I just felt worried that our daily shooting schedule, with a 7 a.m. call and not wrapping up till late, would crowd my workout. The feeling of the hotel's grand luxury made me feel more like an interloper than anything else. I mean who was I supposed to be? I was more at home in a run-down dojo with a few training partners than I would ever be in a place like this. But to keep my life my own I made sure I got up extra early to train. That's why it was 4 a.m. as I began to wander the halls of the place. I found a quiet expanse of floor with no one else around. I trained silently, barefoot on the polished wooden floor, just the sounds of my feet sliding. The sweat began to bead up and pour off me and I felt at home once again. Two hours later the sun was coming up I was still moving through my regular morning kata routine when I saw, between the palm fronds all around me illuminated by the golden dawn, the faces of the guys on the early shift, there in their restaurant to set up for breakfast, but wanting to watch or maybe unsure if they should interrupt this guest or afraid to talk to me, a nut. I said good morning and got out of there as nonchalantly as I could.

I trained in hotel rooms between the beds, converting the long *embusen*—the steps of the kata—to small backward and forward steps to fit the space, still able to feel good and keep sharp, but looking forward to getting to a roof top or hallway for a workout where I could stretch my arms and legs to the limit and just move.

I tried to work out in my apartment, a walk-up, just off Tompkins Square Park, but the neighbors, the nice family with the baby next door, the rode-hard couple across the way, the Nichiren chanters downstairs, all told me they could hear me. One guy came to my door and knocked on it one evening around six. I recognized him through the peephole so I went and unlocked and unbolted the door. He held a hammer above his head, ready to drop it on mine just in case I went mental on him. He was just playing it safe, I thought, as I looked up at the hammer hanging there in his hand, softly, sort of passively above me. I said, "How's it going?" He said, "Good, good," but I was shaking the building and he was trying to relax at home, so would I mind, not, doing… um, whatever I was doing? No problem. So the roof it was. Tarred and spongy, with an 18-inch wall, a little rim of brick around the edges, pools of congealed tar and pools of water in the summer, ice all winter. I had plenty of room to move and I trained up there every morning, rain, snow or ten below zero.

I made sure that I started the day hot, and finished it exhausted. As long as I collapsed completely tired at night I knew that I was getting nearer my goal, and that I would not lie awake listening to my heartbeat or wondering about anything. I knew I had taken a step forward. I had not declined. I had gotten stronger.

Making sure as best I could that I would be unnoticed I trained everywhere I went for two reasons. Partly I trained to stay sharp. Arthur Rubinstein: "If I do not practice for one day I notice. If I do not practice for two days the orchestra notices. If I don't practice for three days, the audience notices." Zen Master Hyakujo: "A day without work is a day without food." To me a day of not practicing was a day of decline.

The other reason I practiced every day was that it humanized the toxic, sterile environments I found myself in. So I practiced. In hidden corners of empty airport gates in the middle of the night. In an unused recording studio down the hall from a session. In a cavernous hangar on an Army base. In a shadowy sound stage. I practiced in solitude along the trails and beaches of New England.

I practiced, slow motion, a few minutes at a time, not breaking a sweat, in a deserted marble hallway of the county court house where I waited forever for my divorce to be done.

A member of my dojo told me that the one time he was arrested was for driving under the influence and he spent the whole night in a cold holding cell alone doing one of his kata, the new one he had just learned that week at the dojo, over and over again. To keep warm, he said.

Your practice is like a totem you carry around with you, only it *is* you.

The beginning of training is something like starting a wood fire. That first spark of enthusiasm has to catch on something, and that something has to be tinder dry and ready to go. And what usually happens at that point is that unless all the conditions are right the tinder burns up hot and bright and it flares out. That is what happened to me with the first few martial arts I tried. That is what happened with most of the people who started at my school in the first few years. Because I could not provide them with the right conditions for that tinder to catch onto something deeper. I wanted to offer them an example of a life of practice, something like the big chunks of hardwood that will burn with a constant flame on and on through the night, untended, all on their own. I was too pre-occupied with my own agenda to inspire them, to show them how their spark of enthusiasm could ignite something profound. I couldn't even get to the first twig a lot of times. I wish I had not been so green myself.

But it worked for some people. There are a few who started then and are still practicing today. It's a collaboration. The student has to bring their desire and the teacher has to give them instruction and respect. I did not know how to do that. Had I associated myself with a great teacher whom I wholeheartedly admired, right from the beginning, it would have gone some other way. But without realizing how compromising the effects would be, I compromised.

A few years into my time in Purgatory, a few years before I came to Northampton to begin my dojo, my training day began with the same words on my lips every day. It was like a mantra: Fuck it.

My mantra was defiant. There were times when, to teach me humility, people broke my bones and smashed my body. Training so furiously—twice a day, seven days a week—I was arrogant and I was disturbing their relationship with the Boss.

I should have noticed it. It's natural. In the world of monkeys and monarchies, for example, individuals define their status in relation to the boss.

In corporate life, turf and access are currency. They are acquired and defended vigorously. Disturbing the peace is discouraged. It makes sense. People moving into new areas are careful to show deference, and not to accidentally transgress unmarked but real boundaries. I wasn't aware of the concerns of the people around me. I wasn't much interested.

In corporate life schmoozing builds trust among strangers. It forms a sense of connection and of common purpose on which careers are built.

By the time I noticed that pain was permeating my experience of Purgatory I had invested years learning the karate there. I could give it up and move on, again, or tolerate the unpleasantness and continue.

So when I said "fuck it" on my way up the stairs each evening
it was my way of saying that no matter how much hazing goes on,
no matter how much violence is in the air, I will just go through
it, and train. Sometimes there was no problem. Sometimes there
was. For a while the thought that there might be was a constant
feature of practicing. Another broken bone? Another hour holding
a stance? "Who cares. Fuck it. I'm training." In a way I was stupid
to put up with it. But by defying my own limits, my attachment to
comfort and to the safety of my body, despite my foolishness or the
shortcomings of that culture, I became stronger. Still, I did not know
if all this effort would pay off, if I would ever be any good at karate,
if this path would lead me... anywhere.

But I said, "Fuck it: I will drop dead on the deck before I back off."

For example, one time the class was lined up in two rows. Each
person was facing a partner. My partner, a former college football
player, now a newly minted stock analyst, was in this class, on
his lunch hour. He had about a year of practice. We were doing a
three step sparring routine in which you know the three moves the
attacker will do and you defend against them. Each person gets
a chance to attack the other and then to defend against the same
attacking sequence.

When the opponents perform the sequence of techniques as
designed, the defender wins. The winning technique is a punch to
the nose of the attacker, which is to be thrown forcefully but stopped
just short of the target. This allows people to practice powerful
techniques with focus but without injury.

In this case the guy was so excited that he failed to pull the winning technique. Instead of stopping it a quarter inch in front of my nose he flattened my nose instead. I heard the crack from inside my head. No one else heard it because at that moment, in time with the final punch, each person emits a *kiai* (a loud shout.) The sound of the kiai's from 20 people masked the cracking sound completely.

Blood flowed down my chin and dripped onto my white uniform. As the movement sequence concluded the two rows of training partners separated. Each person stood a foot or so from their partner, facing them, ready for the next routine to begin.

Breaking protocol, speaking in the silence, the guy whispers to me, "You're bleeding..." and then a little louder, as it if I didn't hear, "You're bleeding..." I stood there, bleeding. I said, "Don't worry about it. Just keep going." And we did. Fuck it.

In those days we did not worry about blood. Now we are careful about it. Incidents involving injury and blood were rare occurrences, then and now. There are fewer injuries in a year-round, ongoing practice like karate than there are in a seasonal sport like tennis, basketball or skiing, where people tend to return to playing after a long layoff and then burst into full-out competition.

In karate we know that anyone can injure anyone. When it happens it usually means that something's gone wrong.

One evening after a workout (this was the mid 1980s, I was a
new black belt) we were all on our way downtown to have dinner at
our favorite spot in Little Italy.

On the way down the stairs from Purgatory we saw two guys,
dark skinned guys, sitting on the stairs leading down from our dojo
to the street. They were on our stairs. They were smoking a joint.
The Boss said to them, in a tone of outraged authority, "What the
fuck are you doing?", and one of them said, "It's none of your
business." And the Boss just hollers back, "Well I'm making it my
fucking business, now get out of my building." and so they did. If
we just walked by the result might have been about the same. They
might have walked out of the building thirty seconds later, or they
might have kicked in the door of an apartment and killed an old
lady, the conversation went. Who knew? But we knew for sure that
he was the Boss. And he got them out of our building.

Walking down the street, cooling down in the night breeze we
started talking, me and him and a few other guys. He always knew
what was what. Someone told him about some outrage at work,
how it made it unpleasant to be there. And he said, "That's why they
call it work. You don't have to go in singing every day. You do your
job. Then you leave."

Cool. He told us what to do if you face a gang. Hit the leader.
Just pick the biggest, baddest one. Take him out, they'll all scatter.
He knew. He'd done it. There was a way to win and he knew it.
And he was right there, in the flesh, willing to share it all with us
for nothing. Just the way older guys have told younger guys how it's
done since the beginning of time.

15. One Light

Karate practice mattered to me more than anything else. My dedication seemed peculiar to some of the people I practiced with at that time because for them karate was a fun exercise or a way to build self-defense skills. From their point of view there wasn't any pay off that could justify my expenditure of energy and time. It was not suave. But I went ahead and burnt up my pain in the fire of training and drowned my demons in sweat.

I had the same intensity when I first opened my dojo, and when students would disappear I wondered if I had let them down. Sometimes people would come to the school expecting aerobics or Bruce Lee and find a thousand punches, and me. I wondered if I wasn't skillful enough to present karate training to them in a way they would understand and welcome and jump into. I got better at reaching people, presenting the side of practice that I thought would appeal to them, seeing the experience more from their point of view, as a newcomer, rather than from my own, filled with assumptions and experiences that didn't match theirs at all.

I wondered about the people who stuck with it. What responsibility did I have to them? And to what degree had I become responsible for them? To what degree was I responsible for the quality of the self-defense skills and the quality of the mental conditions they were cultivating in my dojo?

As I presented it, the training was as intense for them as I had made it for myself. Long, hard training and genuine respect between people is what I wanted. Along with an intelligent consideration of the issues of physical conditioning, energy training, awareness, the ethical and tactical issues of martial arts and the issues of life which seemed to me to be constantly casting light and shadows on each other, and which, for a complete and happy life, ought to be vigorously investigated and completely penetrated.

That was the combination I had not been able to find in any dojo. If I had found it I would have joined up. But I did not. I tried to create the place I imagined. As I did I wondered if I was working hard enough, being awake enough and imaginative enough. And I didn't have a way to answer it.

One frozen February morning about 6 a.m., still dark, the frigid Canadian air swept through the hills of Massachusetts. I was far from civilization, cross-legged on the floor next to a hissing kerosene heater, with a cup of steaming tea set, centered in front of me on the low oak table. The tea was made with water boiled on a smoky rusty old wood stove. The cup of tea steamed for about 30 seconds before the cold air cooled it. I wrapped my hand around the little cup trying to absorb as much of the heat as I could. And across the table sat a Japanese Zen monk, who lived there at that small Zendo in rural Massachusetts a half hour from my house. I met him every Friday morning at 6 a.m. for meditation and discussion, for years.

In those days he lived alone in the woods, just him and his vow. In the winter it was cold. In the summer there was a vegetable garden and a stream of visitors and work to do on the house and the grounds, and miles and miles of woods to walk in every direction. In the winter his daily practice of zazen—two hours every morning and evening, 12 hours every Sunday, a three- or five-day sesshin every month, the same schedule he had kept at Antaiji monastery in the countryside near Kyoto—was pretty much all there was for him.

You could see forever from up there. With the leaves long gone, from the top of that hill, out the small windows of the Zendo dining room, you could see the whole valley, the horizon, a big wide slice of the world. And after the pretension of the big meditation centers I'd been to, the props and procedures, the buildings and grounds, the membership rituals, the marketing, the rules and regulations, the group dynamics, the registrations and the traveling, this place was a true dharma home. The real thing. And this man was living it.

No ads, no fliers, no sales pitches, no fund raising, no dogma, no doctrine, no demands. To me he was prajna paramita embodied, in a placid, agile full lotus position.

Our conversations were elliptical. I did not speak any Japanese, and his English was good enough for getting around but not up to a level where he could communicate the subtlety of his thinking or his range of knowledge. So we kept it simple. Sometimes we kept it confusing. But nevertheless the life there, the meditation, the pure fresh genuine winter cold, the schedule as regular as a heartbeat, his conviction and courage and solitude, were convincing. So when I voiced my concern about whether or not I was living up to my responsibility toward the students I was teaching in my dojo he said "It's their karma. You can't worry about it."

Ah! Thank you. And so I go, once again, down the hill a hundred yards, plunging in my frozen boots step by step through two feet of untrammeled snow squinting in the brilliant morning sunlight to the parking lot to the car down the mountain refreshed, reoriented, ready to return to the regular world. It took a long time for the ice in my shoes to melt on those days. The shoes had been on the floor in the waiting area of the Zendo. There was no heat out there at all. The snow that fell from my cuffs into my warm shoes when I arrived that morning at dawn melted there and then froze inside like Eskimo orthotics. My whole lower body was numb from sitting in the cold for hours. But I was happy with the whole thing as I stopped for coffee at the friendly and familiar gas station at the bottom of the hill, the entry ramp back to civilization.

This monk was completely confident in the piece of advice he gave me. It was sound, not because I was relieved from responsibility, but because I was relieved of useless worry.

I have had many pieces of advice from people over the years. Much of it given with complete confidence. And lots of it wrong. In some cases I followed it, because the speaker had confidence. And it hurt me and hurt other people. So, after it became clear that I was going wrong, I stopped. But how can you tell in advance (when you really need the advice, when you are too new or too young to know for yourself) if the advice is good and true and useful? How can you test the unknown for truth?

16. Severe Training

As a result of all the hard training I did in those years I had
some unusual experiences. I usually trained four hours a day at least,
mostly doing kata. For one year, in addition to my regular class
schedule, I did 100 repetitions of a single kata each day. That took
about an hour and a half. One day during that practice I felt my
body moving without any effort or, it seemed, volition. At a given
point in each kata is a kiai—a shout—during which the energy of
the body is focused and projected into an imaginary target. I felt my
kiai arise by itself without me. It was as if the room was completely
empty, except for the sound of the kiai, which hung in the air for a
long time before dissipating.

Another time a beam of light radiated from the center of my
chest to the sky. That lasted about an hour.

A few weeks later, I spent an afternoon—walking, working,
practicing—with the distinct sensation that every object I looked
at was me, and that I was it. I would look at the sunlight pouring
through some leaves softly moving in the breeze and, enraptured, I
said to myself: "It's me! I am that!"

Another unusual experience came late one night. I was
completely exhausted, alone in the cold dojo, after all the students
had left. There was a bright full moon, it was a clear night, and the
lights were down in the dojo. The moonlight fell in a row of long
shadows on the floor through windows in the old brick wall. I knelt
down on the floor to rest for a minute. Silence came up like a wave
or a sudden cloudburst and overwhelmed me completely. My head

went down toward the floor and my forehead touched the wood, and I was grateful, grateful, grateful.

Years went by with nothing like that happening. Then one day I was practicing for a long time and students began to arrive for class. I continued to practice as the room began to fill up with students arriving for the noon class. I finished a kata and, although I was now surrounded by people training and lots of activity, my own stillness was what I felt most clearly. I had a feeling that walls dissolved. I was overwhelmed with the feeling that things are as they are. Things are as they are! It was a very emotional moment. The words sound unimpressive. They don't convey the experience. But the feeling of freedom was overwhelming.

Those were my unusual shugyo experiences. Shugyo is 'severe training'. It is a kind of martial arts practice that pushes the practitioner to the outermost limits of their endurance. At some point in this training it is necessary to relinquish our attachment to our body and mind and proceed on will and conditioning. Our habit as modern people is to restlessly project ourselves away from the moment we are in. We plan and remember or want and regret, continually. The demands of shugyo bring us directly to the present. Then we are released. There is a feeling of freedom and purity. The experience of liberation that comes from this kind of practice is temporary. There are other training methods that yield lasting freedom.

17. Two Truths

That's a piece of advice: an encouragement to train. It may or may not sound convincing to you. How would you know for sure, before you have first hand experience? The tools we have to use are our faculties of perception, our logical faculty, and the reports of trustworthy people—in this case of master practitioners.

Nagarjuna was a first century Indian Buddhist monk who revived the profound teachings of Buddhism at a time when Buddhism had declined. He taught the doctrine of two truths. He named the two truths 'deceptive truth' and 'truth'.

We assume that the objects in the world around us exist on their own, with fixed qualities of their own. This is a misunderstanding.

There is a deeper truth that takes training to see. Perceiving this truth directly is the central objective of Buddhist practice. Meditation allows the mind to settle down so that our perception and logical faculties can operate without distortion. But no matter how hard we try meditation will only work if we live ethically. If we don't, if we treat others badly, we will have a life filled with conflict and our mind will not settle down enough to meditate. To succeed it is essential to train ourselves in meditation and ethical conduct. This way we can see what causes suffering and how to get rid of suffering.

In Sanskrit the nature of things is described as *sunyatta*. In English it is translated as 'emptiness'. This is a technical philosophical term, with a meaning different from the conventional use of the word in English.

To understand it we have to ask, "What is it that phenomena are supposed to be empty of?"

According to Buddhist philosophy phenomena are empty of fixed characteristics that exist on their own independently. In fact things exist dependent upon 1. The causes and conditions that brought the thing into existence; 2. The parts that constitute it now; and 3. The predisposition of the mind that perceives the phenomenon.

That predisposition is formed by our karma. Karma is not fate, luck or chance. Our karma—i.e. our mental habits formed by our past actions of body, speech and mind—forces us to see things through the filter of our experience. If we change our behavior— what we do, what we say, how we think—then little by little our world will change. If we act virtuously the world becomes more beautiful. If we act cruelly the world becomes uglier and suffering increases. Karma works because reality is empty of a fixed nature of its own. The implication of this for training is that if we learn what actions result in putting an end to suffering and we train ourselves to take those actions vigorously and consistently, we can end suffering for ourselves and others.

Deceptive truth is the world we see, a world that appears to us to be true on its own. We see objects we think will bring us happiness or unhappiness. We fail to understand the way in which the qualities of those objects are reflections of our own mind. We act on the basis

of that misunderstanding and so perpetuate suffering for ourselves
and for others.

How do we stop doing that? How do we test our own perceptions
for truth? We are presented with assertions of truth. By friends and
family, politicians and salesmen, books and TV and movies. Many
of these assertions are untrue. A child in the middle of the night sees
a belt in the shadows in the floor. You hear: "A snake! A snake!" He
is sincerely scared. His heart is racing. So is yours.

He didn't simply imagine the snake. His mind was programmed
to watch out for snakes by a few hundred million years of evolution,
a successful survival strategy hardwired into his brain. But now he
was deceived, misunderstanding the nature of what he saw with his
own two eyes.

To many people a gambling casino looks like fun. A career on
Wall Street may seem to offer a secure life. To a drunk a drink will
look like a source of pleasure. They aren't. To a racist the presence
of the member of another race is vile. The mistaken conclusion
that people make in all these cases is to presume the qualities they
identify as desirable or undesirable are inherent in the object, not
a function of their mind. Then they try to obtain what appears
desirable and eliminate what seems undesirable.

The result is that people's minds are endlessly disturbed, trying
to manipulate objects that they misunderstand, and not getting the
results they want. You get ethnic cleansing. Robbery. Advertising.
Drug addiction. Traffic. Infidelity. War. The list is endless as waves
on an ocean.

The fact that all things exist in dependence upon their causes, their parts and our perceptions does not mean that anything goes. It means that everything is subject to influence and change. It means that everything we do, say and think has a consequence which boomerangs right back to us. It means that through sincere training we can put an end to suffering.

18. Five Dollars

In my 20s and 30s karate practice was a welcome respite from turbulent emotions and thinking. What a relief it was to be able to just shut up and train. It felt honest. It provided a stark contrast to graduate school and to ad agency life. Even 7 or 8 years into my training career I was still unable to invent the life I wanted, or even to clearly imagine it.

I came up with assemblages, parts that I cobbled together to produce what I thought would be a workable life. I got started at the ad agency as a result of karate. It was the mid-eighties. I wrote the dojo newsletter. An executive at an ad agency across the street, who trained at that dojo on his lunch hour, read the newsletter and asked who is writing this? Someone pointed me out. Ah hah. What did I do for a job? I was in graduate school. Why not stop by his office after graduation. I did.

During the years before I went to graduate school I had written for a living on and off. When I worked as a roadie for a band on tour, in a crew on an all-night delivery truck, I wrote every day. Those were the pieces I used in my grad school application.

The years I spent in the program I could hardly write at all. During those years I practiced karate, furiously. I walked. I explored the architecture of the public parts of the city. I knew them well. Every block, every store, every lot. I escaped the city streets by walking along the rivers. There you could see the sky and the titanic city itself. I walked under the vaulting spans supporting the roads above and concealing strange people below. These places became familiar turf to me. I could breathe fresh air off the river, and be in an environment not built but Created.

In my office I felt constricted by the information underload of the synthetic physical environment, hemmed in by the buildings and streets that made that world. I yearned for expanse. For the endlessly searchable, mysterious, changing, sensible information flood of the natural world. Why could I not imagine my way out to the world beyond the fabricated environment bounded by advertising, media, personal ambition, delight and dread? Out of the human urban world whose shape and sound is a cascade of wanting, wanting, wanting. Because that world was my mind reflected?

In contrast the karate dojo looked like paradise. Depending on your perspective Purgatory can be a step up. Hope was there, everywhere I looked. It was made out of natural things, wood and plaster and brick, and the touch of human hands were all over it. I saw the flow of human life in the cracks in the plaster, the gaps between the mismatched boards, the leaks in the ceiling. The cracks, patched and filled in and broken out a hundred times over the decades, showed signs of imperfect life that were banished from the antiseptic corporate buildings where I spent my days.

There the polished cool marble, the acres of carpet, the uniform white walls, the flawless drop ceilings, the hush, the well-hung fine art, felt suffocating. There was no way into it. I felt like a pet. Clear rules. Praise or penalty. It was a way to support my training, I told myself. I compromised and naturally, was compromised as a result.

In the dojo I was free to be alive, with every gesture every thought, every new technique, every drop of sweat, every silent pause, toward perfection. Nothing wasted. No one deceived.

And there was a room full of people who shared it all. I did not know most of them, but there we were showing up at the same time, day after day, week after week, doing the same moves, shouting as loud as we could, smashing our fists into the thin air again and again till, as the months went by, we could hear the thick cotton sleeves of our jackets snap with every punch, we could hear the walls reverberate and the floor yielding with a satisfying shudder every time we slammed our feet into the well worn wooden boards.

I felt like one of the trees that sprouts between the cracks of the sidewalk in abandoned parts of town, that grows up and splits the pavement all the way across and then, with good luck, can just grow up and push the concrete aside and have a life, even there. That's what I felt like. Too melodramatic? There are times when you need stark contrast to create motion. Like flint and steel. Like lightning. Like true love.

As I pressed with all my effort onto this one point, breaking away from the world of art with all its feelings, sharing, posturing, desire, yearning and sensitivity, the need and the fear and the talking, and the ever-present promise of gratification lurking always just beyond the horizon, I wanted out. I was trying to break out, to break through to something alive and better and true. But with all that single-mindedness I lost sight of my objective (a free and honest life) and focused only the method: I became narrow and hardheaded.

Two guys came up to me on a busy corner, and pressed against me on both sides. They appeared from the midst of the crowd while we were all waiting for the light to change. One of these two tall guys, faces so close to mine that I could smell them, spoke.

It should have set off an alarm in my mind when, seconds before, I walked past a guy lying on the sidewalk, bleeding and groaning. I thought little of it. It was not unusual for that place and time. The sight of people laying down on the sidewalk, especially in the warm weather, was common. There were people lying on the pavement, on metal grates, at the side doors of office buildings, or in the little square patches of dirt cut out from the cement sidewalk around the trees, a bag of belongings or a shopping cart full of cans by their side.

So here was another one, nothing special, he blended in. But this particular guy on the ground was bleeding. And he was not dressed in rags. The signs were not subtle. But they were too subtle for me. Because I was so used to being single-minded and determined I overdid it this time. I just kept going.

When I got to the corner these two big guys came up to me, one on each side. And one pushed into me to get my attention. When I looked over he slipped a screwdriver from his coat pocket, just enough to let me see what was what. The end was filed to a point. And then the other fellow pressed into me and said "We want five dollars."

They knew, for sure, they could stick that screwdriver into me in an instant and be gone. I knew it too. They knew that I would probably just fall on the ground and moan and bleed like that other guy, and everyone would walk by, relieved they'd dodged this bullet, because we had a habit of being fatalistic about the dangers of our city and we told ourselves you never know when your number's up.

But I just stood there. I did not flinch. I did not care. This was a moment in which my stupidity paid off. I do not recommend this. I recommend giving the money. But I was too short tempered to do that myself so I put my life on the line for the five bucks.

They said "We want five dollars," and I said: "Fuck you you're not getting it." I took one step back and felt sure I could smash one of these guys before the other one killed me and I think the guys thought the same thing, or maybe they just figured, Who needs this headache because there are other people in this crowd who will go along. Whatever the reason they just immediately drifted away into the crowd and they were gone and I went on and I noticed as I crossed 14th Street that my heartbeat was steady as a rock.

19. The Hells

According to Buddhist cosmology, when beings first arrive in hell, they appear there fully formed. If they had done great harm but not the worst kinds, they may land at the first level of hell. There, they are afraid of everyone, hate everyone, and everyone they meet feels the same way about them. Their immediate impulse is to smash each other. If they can pick up a rock or a stick or a weapon they use that. If all they have is their hands and feet, they use them. And what brings them there to this hell? The mental habit of wanting to destroy beings; by having led a life in which they cultivated hatred and rage, having encouraged it or acted on it by hurting and killing others. Is this what we are cultivating in the martial arts?

We do the opposite. We eliminate negative emotions. It doesn't happen by being mellow or by just acting nice. But it is possible to purify your mind of anger through karate practice.

Our bodies and our minds are precious. We ought to take care of them. To do that we need proper food and rest. We also need to think in a healthy way and to treat others well. And if someone attacks us and we cannot avoid their assault then we ought to be able to protect ourselves. If we have neglected our responsibility to ourselves and to others, we lose. If we avoid the hard work it takes to mature as a human being, if we tolerate anxiety and weakness, then we lose our lives, and not just in the event of a conflict.

20. Nothing to Lose

One of Japan's archetypal figures was the samurai, strategist and poet, Miyamoto Musashi. He lived in the 17th century, fought many battles, and killed many opponents. According to legend, after a long career in battle and contest, he went off and lived in solitude, recording his understanding of swordsmanship in a manuscript that is still influential today: *The Book Of Five Rings*. In this compendium of advice for martial artists Musashi says it takes a 1,000 days to forge the spirit and 10,000 to polish it.

During the first phase of a life of practice, the first '1,000 days', we are adding to our store of knowledge, strength and skills.

In the first phase of karate training you learn new techniques, become acquainted with tactics, adopt a new vocabulary and discover new capacities of your body and mind. For that period of time the emphasis is on the additive aspect of training.

Sometimes people get stuck in this phase and assume that developing as a martial artist means continually accumulating. Their karate life focuses on accumulating information—about techniques, methods, styles, teaching lineages, terminology. They may study half a dozen styles or more, switching back and forth from one to the next over the course of days or years. They devote the time they would have used for practice to comparing techniques and other aspects of these different traditions. But where does this kind of accumulation lead?

We miss the chance to master a martial art. Our time is limited. Mastery comes from practice. Not 'knowing about' it, but doing it, and changing as a result. You cannot practice effectively without learning the fundamentals. And new insights will arise throughout your life of practice. But you will not experience the deeper transformation that comes as a result of real practice, if you concentrate too long on accumulation.

Musashi points this out. The second phase in Musashi's description, the 10,000 days, is the polishing and forging. Polishing is a negative process. It requires a lot of energy. If you have ever polished some hard, tough material like metal or marble you know how much energy it takes. And it takes faith in the efficacy of that effort, since the results come slowly and, at first, imperceptibly. Polishing is removing the stuff that obscures the real nature of the material. Forging is transforming the quality of the material itself.

In polishing a human spirit, in the second, 10,000-day phase, there is also a transformation underway. That is, in deeply 'polishing the spirit' we are changing the quality of our body and mind.

When we practice we use our intention to repeatedly put the body and mind under precisely calibrated pressure. Our muscles, tendons, organs and bones change in substance—becoming tougher, more resilient and more our own. Our minds changing in character as well—an almost alchemical transformation from dull to quick, from scattered to focused, from volatile to stable.

When an untrained person undergoes high pressure (in a self-defense situation or a personal crisis, for example) they lose their composure. When an untrained person undergoes very low pressure (a long period of meditation, a long wait in an airline terminal, or an unstructured vacation) their mind tends to behave like a bunch of bats—scattered, unruly, subject to inner impulse and stimulation.

Having practiced for a while we sense that our mind and body have undergone a transformation. If we look at this process more deeply, we can glimpse our true nature.

This phrase 'true nature' can sound like it means "what we are really like inside." It means not 'what we are'—not our physical substance or psychological mechanics, as if to imply that these things have a fixed character of their own. Rather it means that we exist as beings in every way susceptible to transformation through the alchemy of our own action.

It is possible for anyone to get a strong body and a focused mind as a result of training. Anyone can learn self-defense. But the more clearly we understand the process the more we are able to get the profound results that are the worthy goal of a life of practice.

21. Welcome to Purgatory

I was on my way to meet my friends one warm July afternoon. Recently graduated from college and living in New York, most of us worked at night, in theaters and nightclubs, concert halls and on movie sets. During the day we had extra time. That day I threaded my way through the traffic-choked streets of midtown.

I saw a sign for a karate school and I went in. I had already checked out many other places. I had tried half a dozen other styles. I went into this karate school mostly on force of habit. I had lost my high hopes. Karate wasn't really the kind of martial art I was looking for. But there I was with extra time, so I went in.

I watched a group of people doing kata, unison fighting movement sequences. Their faces ran with sweat. Their white uniforms were soaked. They stood in rows, at attention, in several geometrically arranged groups, wearing different colored belts. They stood tall, eyes straight-ahead, motionless. They looked determined. Unfazed by the heat or the demands of their effort. At the sound of a shouted command they began again. Their unison motion, the unison rush and snap of their uniforms as they moved, the unison shouts at one point in their drills gave me the impression they had extraordinary discipline and self control.

They were strong. Men and women, different ages, different sizes, all doing this same thing together. I want to do this. But then: I don't know how! That was the main problem. Everyone already knew what to do.

So I talked it over with Pete, one of the guys there, and he told me it was simple: We'll show you what to do. Yeah, you should definitely do it. I love it, he said. You'll learn it.

I haven't missed a day of training since then. And of all the thousands of members who arrived at that school, and at mine, and joined and stayed and trained for a few months, a few years, a few decades, and then disappeared, from that school and from the school I started years later, there are some people who have been partners in training all this time. I still train with Pete.

One time Pete and a few others were sitting in a pizza place down the block from the dojo, when three kids casually walked behind him and stole his gym bag. They ran out of the pizza place with his bag. Pete chased them. He tackled them all and took his bag back, and when the cops came over a second later he said the three of them tripped, and the cops said fine.

There was a good feeling of practical skill in the class I watched that day. But it was the method of achieving it, kata, which convinced me.

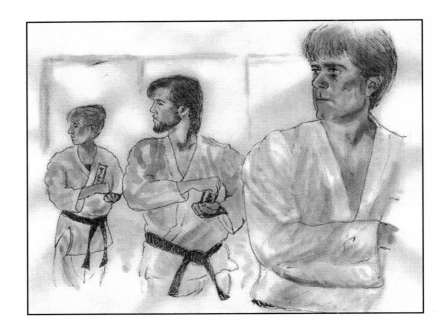

22. Kata

A badly made kata, or one distorted in transmission from one generation to the next, is not worth much. And while at first you may have to take on faith that a particular kata is an authentic and great one, after some practice, you can discern for yourself the qualities that make the traditional kata a set of exquisitely refined training tools. Properly understood and skillfully used, they work.

You can use kata to get healthy, to get strong, to develop tactical skill, to produce a great flow of energy in your body, to transmit energy explosively into a target, to sense the motion of an opponent, to harness your body and mind, to integrate them, and to attain freedom.

23. Unwrapping the Mysterious Package

The black belt arrived just on time on a gray winter day. *Oku Myo Zai Ren Shin*. "Deep reality exists in training the heart and mind," Sakiyama Roshi was saying to me. We had discussed it in detail months before. These were the words that hung on the scroll on the front wall of his teacher's dojo.

Did he know, somehow, the details of my daily life? Was it a coincidence?

He called it an 'en'. En literally means a 'condition.' It is half of the Japanese phrase 'in/en' meaning causes and conditions. The 'in' is the proximate cause, the last straw, the key that turns the ignition switch to start the car. It can also be the material cause: the acorn that produces the oak tree. This 'in' functions because there is a vast collection of en, the underlying conditions, which must all be in place in order, for example, for the car to start and run when the key turns in the ignition, or when, after many years of training, a karate practitioner can 'suddenly' break a stack of bricks with his hand.

According to Sakiyama Roshi, he and I shared a strong karmic connection and so we should not be surprised at all by this kind of coincidence. Two minds encountering each other like two arrows meeting in mid air. Apparently two different causes but really arising from a single cause, he implied. Unlikely, yet there we were.

And there I was. Half a world away receiving his message wrapped in brown paper and tied with a string. There were two belts were inside, not just the one with Oku Myo Zai Ren Shin on it.

The Chinese characters on the other one read: *Ken Zen Ichi Nyo*, "Karate and Zen as One." The calligraphy that hangs behind Shoshin Nagamine in his portrait on the cover of his book *The Essence of Okinawan Karate Do*. In that photograph he is seated in full lotus position, eyes half closed, wearing a white karate uniform, sitting as we had that morning years ago, in front of his dojo shrine. Maybe he was in that posture that very moment, at dawn on Okinawa.

I didn't know Shoshin Nagamine well. I knew him only as a human being who had overcome difficulty and suffering and who, through generosity and strength, had given generations of Okinawan karate practitioners what they needed.

This was something worth doing. Even if I could not achieve it on the scale he did, at least I could aim my life in that direction.

24. Every Move You Make

There are plenty of alternative explanations that describe how our lives take shape. But none as complete as *karma*. Karma in Sanskrit means action. It includes what we do, say and think, and to the results that come from what we do, say and think. And as we penetrate more deeply into the subject it reveals the way our actions condition the way we see the world and how we live our lives.

Karma does not deny the function of personal psychology. It places it in a meaningful and more explanatory context. Consider the idea that we make our life choices in an effort to overcome some early trauma. This theory of psychological compensation explains very little. The reasons why certain conditions came together to produce the initial difficulties in the life of this particular person, the way that person responds, that individual's ultimate triumph over it or their failure to triumph, the happiness or misery that results, the effect the example has on others, why similar childhood conditions work out in very different ways in different lives—none of that is persuasively explained by the mechanics of personal psychology.

How about brain chemistry? One glorious Saturday afternoon in autumn a group of divorced soccer dads were standing around at the sidelines during a game. Between plays they were discussing their divorces, their finances, their fiancées, and the events that brought them to their present state. It was a nice chance to hang out. They talked about their first wives. The tyranny, pettiness, the emotional vacuum, the injustice, the legal troubles, the expense, the children....

One fellow explained that his troubles started with his amygdala. "It's primitive and powerful, and when that baby kicks in, forget about it," he said. Who could blame him for clinging to that little almond-shaped gland while his ship sank? He grasped it as a way to explain away free will and personal responsibility. Like the great puppeteer in the sky, the man behind the curtain, here was the homunculus, the little man at the center of his pre-determined universe. By selecting secretions as the explanation he could take himself out of the game of his own life, and stand on the sidelines for a while.

It may go some way toward explaining how, but that is as far as this explanation can go, no matter how detailed it becomes. It does not explain why we do what we do.

'How' is for science. 'Why' is for metaphysics. Take the example of two people in a car that crashes. One dies. A kid asks, "Why." An engineer or a doctor can answer about the design of the car, the surface of the road, the angle of the impact, the body of the victim: explanations of how. But why one died and the other lived is not a question amenable to scientific analysis.

There are enough innocent sufferers all over the world, who's actions we might judge to be good or bad, who are young and old, rich and poor, black and white, and so on, in infinite variation, to justify putting real effort into a search for an answer to 'Why?'

Here are four answers: 1. An external will. 2. Meaningless chance. 3. Mechanical determinism. 4. The operation of karma.

These are hard to test for truth simply by tracing the sequence of causes that led to the result, because we do not have access to the vast constellation of causes for any event. However, as a starting point, we can test each one of these pragmatically. We can examine the results a person will get if he chooses any one of these four as an assumption on which to base his life choices. They will result in different ways of living.

The first, done in an unhealthy way, can lead to passivity, dread and magical thinking. Undertaken in a healthy way it can lead to giving up egotism and dedicating one's self to prayer and good works, for the sake of peace in this world and the hope of reward in the future.

The second (a belief that the world is governed by meaningless chance) can lead to pleasure seeking, impulsiveness, anxiety, depression, yearning, and an abdication of personal responsibility. Dice hanging from the rear-view mirror, when your number's up your number's up.

The third assumes that because our fates are foreordained there is nothing we can do but ride the train and see what station we arrive at. It takes your life out of your hands and makes people nervous or pompous or passive.

The fourth gives you both the responsibility and the means to take control of your life and make of it what you want. If you act virtuously, you have as happy a life as you can possibly have. Every action, of your body, speech and mind, counts. Nothing is wasted.

My karma—the actions that I take now and the actions I took in the past—constitute my life. Therefore I should, as well as I can, examine my motivation for action, the quality of the action I take, and the results of each thing I do, say, or think. Then I can tell if my action will bring happiness or unhappiness to me and to others. This is why practice works.

Our actions affect the quality of our own lives. We also teach as we live. We influence everyone we come in contact with for good or ill. We may never know how far our influence may spread.

If this were a simple matter of our influence on others working like a closed, physical system, like ripples on the surface of a pond, our effects could be discounted because with each new ripple, echo, or person influenced, a little of the initial energy would be dissipated. And eventually the karmic energy will dissipate and our effect will be gone. But it doesn't work that way. Karma is as likely to magnify as is to dissipate, depending on the conditions of the minds it touches.

For example: You are riding along in your car and you accidentally cut someone off, or they think you did, while you are changing lanes to exit. They become enraged. They speed up, give you the finger, and start chasing you down the exit ramp.

Their action will affect you. You can stay cool. When the nut pulls up beside you you wave and say, "Sorry, sorry, I didn't see you." Then the guy says, "Watch what you're doing asshole," and drives away.

Or: he chases you down the exit ramp, and you have had it up to here. You get angry. You get out of your car, he gets out of his car, and fists or bullets fly, and one of you is dead and one is arrested. Same set up, but with a different mind state for one person. That produces a different action and a different outcome for the two of them, their families, and who knows how many others.

The fates of nations depend on mental habits and choices like these.

Why was the first person able to drive away calmly, no big deal, where the second person felt compelled to get into a confrontation over it? The same conditions were present.

The difference was karma: action in the present time, and the results of past actions in the form mental tendencies that manifest in the present.

We teach how to be all the time. Whether we intend to or not. People see us act in a volatile manner, they will learn from it. If we are in a position of responsibility or power then our actions will more likely be noted and taken seriously, and imitated. So we all have a responsibility that extends far beyond our own lives. We can have a wonderful effect on people. We will certainly have some effect. We ought to take that responsibility seriously. In the dojo we have an opportunity to put this idea into practice every day.

25. The Music of Purgatory

When we are getting started in life we feel our way. Our past
karma is manifesting. Continuing at the first dojo I stuck with
was like listening to the band Procol Harum with my roommates
in college. Out of those huge clouds of sound pouring out of the
Hammond B3 organ, vibrato billowing in every direction, life turned
for a few minutes backlit in gold and blue. Out of the cumulus sound
of their music I felt as if I looked down on from the window of an
airplane at 30,000 feet, from the top of Everest, or from heaven.
And from out of the blue way up there came the voice of, who?, I
never knew the name of the singer. It was the Procol Harum guy.
Maybe that was his name. No, no. The name had a meaning. I never
thought to look it up, I thought, "Someday, I'll know it." The voice,
sincere, gritty, holding back all the pain all the truth he had seen.
His sound grabbed our hearts with his fervor and his universe-filling
blues. We caught the updraft and reluctantly had to agree that yes,
yes, yes, that was it all right. He knows about it. All the emotion
that now seems histrionic, felt accurate at the time. I never had any
idea what the song was about. But it hinted at something treasured
lost, some innocence gone and never ever recoverable, something
vulnerable hurt, something sweet gone ironic, once darling now out
for number one, or something like that, who knows, and I never in
my wildest imagination, although I heard the song a thousand times,
imagined that in the words, "We skipped a light fandango," he might
have been talking about sex, drugs, rock'n roll, ambition, courting,
dancing or anything in particular. It was a feeling. My mind
searched the lyrics for meaning. The memory of a love affair gone
gone gone… The incoherent scribbling of an intoxicated English
major, echoing a line from Hamlet, recalling something he heard

about Chaucer and Roman religion... And all those virgins leaving for the coast, and his face once ghostly... something was going from bad to worse... Loss, self-pity, yet soldiering on despite it all. Or was it secretly about Clapton and Paul McCartney? But in the song the girl was suffering this loss or pain or disappointment, like the moment when you tell her goodbye, and you say, "This feels worse to me than it does to you," all that seemed familiar. The meaning would hover over the lyrics even though the lyrics didn't actually say anything of the kind, her face at first just ghostly, turned a whiter, shade of pale.... And off goes that solo reaching for majesty posturing like a teenager who thinks that no one understands but who in fact everybody completely understands and has understood since the get go. But still, at that moment, at that time, at the sound of that instrumental bridge, I felt compelled to rise to my feet, eyes red rimmed, jaw clenched tight, teeth together, head held high, so moved, doing what I had to do, despite it all despite, what, I don't know... and I said to myself as the sound of the Procol Harum guy's voice pierced the glorious clouds of that Hammond with the Leslie speaker's two double wizard hats spinning in its real wood cabinet and the next verse came soaring up through it all, a sea of regret, longing and eternal determination to rise above the pain, I wanted to stand proud and tall for all times. And although I had no idea what the song was about or what the singer was saying, I still felt completely moved and convinced beyond a shadow of a doubt that the song had meaning. Whatever it might be. And not the measly, commonplace meaning adults might 'understand,' but you know, Meaning.

And in a way that is what my experience in martial arts was like at first.

The lyric is vague. The emotion of the music is clear. The feelings the music produces are easy to project onto the open template of the words. For a few years it was enough to believe that I belonged to something special.

How hard is it to fool people and hurt them? Not hard. How hard is it to inspire people and help them?

26. Pet or Meat?

Tournament Day. Men and women in karate uniforms have been waiting all day in the high school gym for their chance to compete. They warm up. There's a knot in the pit of their stomach. The announcer's voice booms out over the microphone and dissolves into echoes. It's hard to tell who the announcer is calling. You, the competitor, move through the crowd of kids and families who are there for the excitement and you tell yourself this is about a quest for excellence, it's about being the best, or about being your best, or about getting out there and doing it, it's about the thrill of it.

You feel the rush of adrenaline stepping in to the ring. Winning, you feel the raw, primitive surge of power when the impact of your punch makes a strong man crumble. Losing, you feel raw rage, pain as you collapse to the mat, face swelling, bleeding, chest heaving. The silent inner howl of shame and desperation, the vow to never let this happen again, to come back, to come back stronger, to become unbeatable.

Down the block or on the other side of town someone vows to move to the corner office on the 52nd floor, past all the others who wanted it.

He knows and we know that a winner's world is a wonderful world. You notice the whole new level of respect you get from people who yesterday saw you as a colleague, a competitor, a junior guy, as the kind of person they could ask for a ride from the station. Now, in one day, all that has changed.

There are tournaments every weekend. Hundreds of corporations promote people to new jobs, every day. There are endless hierarchies, reward systems, small ponds with big fish. Some rewards have meaning only in a small arena. But some rewards transcend this.

If you check the results and you see that your action did benefit yourself and others, then it was worthy, and will have consequences that will ripple out beyond the boundaries of the group.

But any group's values over time can influence the values of the individuals in it who aim to succeed within the value system of that group. So we have to watch out for which groups we join. It is easy to buy into an arbitrary reward system. Wall Street people say "Money is just a way of keeping score." Could intelligent people really be satisfied with this?

Even if you grow up and outgrow the values that attracted you to a particular group, you have a tendency to stay put. Out of expedience it is easier to stay where you are and justify your actions than it is to find a new pursuit that would be more suitable. I might say: I will do a great job and get ahead. I am part of the team. I will do it because I have responsibilities to my family. I will do it because I only have a few years left to retirement.

Tournaments can be fun. Working in a corporate setting can be useful. But if what we are asked to do is wrong or harmful it cannot be justified as an expedient. If you consciously select and enter into a reward system that fosters virtue then you can pursue that wholeheartedly, and everything you do will be rewarded. Even if no one ever knows what you are doing. That is why a practice is so useful, and why no rank, title or money can substitute for it.

The dojo made sense. No need for moral equivocation to have success there. I wanted to carry a dojo around on my back like a turtle, live in one, make my life into one. Then I do not have to deceive anyone, manipulate anything. Then I will be able to do every action for its own sake and so, win or lose, everything I do will succeed.

27. Wild Life

When I was going to churches and religious centers, listening to lectures, there was a point in each talk where I felt like asking the speaker: Do you know what you are claiming? Or are you just hoping? I was searching for an understanding that was complete, coherent and testable at each point.

One of the descriptions of the suffering of animals in the Abhidharma, a part of the ancient Buddhist literature, is the animals' perpetual fear and need. Those of us in modern society may have a sentimental view of animal life, influenced by movies, cartoons and pets. But in the animal world there are no laws, no restrictions on impulse.

What would that kind of life be like? What would it be like if we went to the supermarket to get dinner because we feel hungry and as we walk down the aisle, instead of picking out some frozen vegetables to put in our cart we just look for someone smaller than us to eat, and when we find someone who is smaller, and more or less healthy, we don't say, "Hello," but instead if we were animals we would just sneak up quietly behind them and jump on them and rip their flesh off and eat them. All the while afraid that someone bigger than we are is about to do the same to us. As human beings we ought to care for animals and to treat them kindly. But because of their condition they take life and are helpless to change.

We humans can understand what will bring happiness to us and to others. We need to learn what to do and then we need to do it. Animals do not have this ability.

We cannot conjure up a primitive state of grace and live in it. Many utopian experiments ended up as evil empires. They thought they had it figured out. There is a temptation in some groups to rely on intuition and guesswork to find a path to a good life. Especially if one has been exposed to deception by authorities in religious life, or in a martial arts dojo, we may feel an even stronger inclination to just improvise based on hunches and hope. This is a mistake since honest, tested and testable instruction is available.

Some deranged nations, political cultures, organizations, even martial arts groups, cultivate negative mental states because greed, anger, jealousy, hatred, and envy energize them and help them to form a sense of purpose and identity. They hope these emotions will tighten the boundaries of the group, to keep members loyal, and alternative ideas and powers at bay.

At first it seems to work. But soon, like survivalists in underground bunkers, rarely seeing anyone or the daylight, their paranoia gets worse, not better, they feel more fearful, not safer, because of the barriers to the world which they erected.

The legacy of Stalin, Hitler and the acts of a thousand little dictators, arrogant, tormented terrorists and self-righteous haters, present us with evidence of the exponential growth of karmic seeds into karmic results. They began hating some people, finding some groups a threat, and ended by hating more and more, until no one is above suspicion, everyone is a threat. Total misery, not safety came out of it. You would think that it would occur to them that if you killed more and more people, more and more people would not only fear you, but they would hate you, too. But they seemed not to grasp the failure of their strategy, or the futility of their cause.

At first being part of a tribe makes you feel bigger and stronger than you feel when you think you are a lone individual. This is one of the attractions of being in a gang. Cults depend on this strong, primitive psychology. It is intoxicating and its misuse is what to watch out for when leading or joining a group.

28. Mirror of Mind

Several of us were doing an all day meditation retreat: periods of sitting meditation alternating with periods of walking meditation. It was warm. The windows were open. We heard the river and the wind blowing the leaves off the oaks outside. The breeze blew the jasmine scent of the incense through the room. Time after time the wind subsided and silence returned. Each hour the solemn sound of the timekeeper's bell marked the start and then the end of the meditation period. We like these sounds.

Then we hear a car's starter motor struggle. Again and again. Someone's in the parking lot. The engine won't start. They shout out to their friend: "Hey! Joanne! It won't start." Silence returns. Then a truck with a diesel engine pulls up. The engine is roaring. The radio is playing a rap song. We feel the bass in our legs, in our chests. The jasmine breeze is replaced by diesel exhaust. The sound blocks out our lovely sensations of oneness with the natural world, pureeing our peace of mind. We don't like this.

It is useful to recall that when the karmic seeds that produced the event are exhausted, the event will vanish. Useful to recall that the events are not merely happening out there, to me in here, but rather that I am a part of the event, a participant in it. Would it produce a more peaceful moment to manipulate every sight, sound, scent, taste, touch and thought or to not split from the reality of that moment, to use that moment's content as the reality of our life and just train?

We are not separate from the impressions and the events of our life.

At my first meditation retreat years before, on one of my many visits to the Zen center in the Catskills, the time came when, after a few days of sitting, my legs were blazing with pain. My muscles were exhausted and my body was shuddering with fatigue. My back was bending and my knees were lifting up. My legs were trained to hold a low stance for a long time, well-conditioned for dropping down and springing up, but not for being folded for long. At this retreat the teacher kept saying, "Don't separate from your pain! Be one with it!" I tried it. In a few seconds I'm thinking, "Forget that, this doesn't work! Okay I'm one with it. It's still killing me!" A few minutes later: "I don't wanna be one with, it I want to stand up and leave."

In fact you are one with it: your body, your perception of pain, your reaction to it all arise together. They are not the same but they are not 'separate.' That gives you a powerful way to deal with suffering. It is not advice. It is a description of reality.

If we find ourselves in a toxic situation—a bad job, a bad relationship, a bad choice—with the insight that the difficulty is our own reflection, we can get out of it by changing the only thing we have the power to change: our actions—what we do, what we say, how we think.

Having joined a group, having attained a position in a hierarchy; we want to rise. We aspire to the rewards that are offered within the framework of the group, and we make effort to avoid the penalties. Inevitably we discover that the rewards are not always attainable and the penalties are not always avoidable. The others whom we first thought of as associates, as a community, or as a team, now appear to us to be competitors for scarce rewards. Our boss or seniors in the hierarchy make us feel envious. We want their job. But we need their favor to get ahead. So we try to get it. Our juniors don't appear to us to be as skillful or as reliable as we want them to be. They flatter us and think we can't tell. They slack off. They try to get something for nothing. We can't respect them completely. And they want our job. What looked like a well organized harmoniously functioning whole, now looks, after a few months or a few years, like pit of intrigue—a world where goals keep receding toward a distant horizon no matter how far you go and how hard you work. And the wanting never ends.

So, as a member of a group, where do the boundaries between 'us' and 'them' stand? They do not stand. The boundaries keep moving, as long as our minds do.

Not everyone is at everyone's throats all the time. But the habit of drawing and redrawing the boundary between us and them, between myself and others, is a reflexive response to shifting emotions.

The response is fast and placement of boundaries is very fluid. Move to a new city, root for a new team. We all have our reasons.

There are people in war zones and wastelands all over the world that feel that it is right to pass on the pain or to stomp on the 'inferior tribes' or the 'others' who were in competition with 'us.'

In the 13th century Genghis Khan said, "The greatest pleasure in life is to defeat your enemies, to chase him before you, to see his cities reduced to ashes, to rob him of his wealth, to see those dear to him bathed in tears, and to clasp to your breast his wives and daughters." It could be considered human nature, if we operate on the premise that we as individuals stand separate from and in opposition to the rest of the world. But we don't in fact, only in habit of mind. The boundaries shift but the mental state of separation continues. And the result is suffering.

If in exchange for power, in the hope of security and happiness, we give up responsibility for our own lives, then we give up our freedom and the group will dictate the terms of our lives. This is what Zen master Sawaki Roshi called group stupidity. It is the enemy of genuine spiritual life.

One sign we can use to detect a martial arts group that has succumbed to group stupidity is the people in the group say only their way is the true way. They say or imply that other systems are bad and lesser and anyone who disagrees with this is ignorant and not 'us' but 'them.' People who accept this nonsense accept it out of their own egotism and fear. People who accept it do not test it for truth. They want confidence but they haven't done the work to attain it. So instead they get truculence in its place.

It's the same in professional life. Giving 100% is essential— with the right motivation and the right objective. It is one thing to motivate people to do their utmost for the sake of saving lives, for example. It harms people if you use the very same words of inspiration to get them to sell more $200 sneakers. The reason we respond the same way to both is because persuasive leaders evoke a feeling we all long for—shared purpose—in a description of the world—us and them—we easily accept.

To some it's cops and assholes. To others the boundary that actually is real is racial. Yes, it's blacks and whites. Light skin, dark skin. Northern and Southern. Race. Class. Gender. Christians and Jews. Arabs and Jews. Christians and Muslims. Catholic and Protestant. Baptist and Methodist. Muslims and Hindus. Shi'a and Sunni. Sephardim and Ashkenazim. Orthodox and Conservative. New Age and Traditional. The conservative wing and the liberal wing. Democratic and Republican. And on and on, endlessly, and always in flux.

The distinctions we often regard as residing inherently in objects do not have boundaries that exist independent of our thoughts. The distinctions do function. But they depend on our thoughts for their existence. However you personally are going to draw the line around yourself, that day, that week, that decade, that lifetime, in whatever way that you think it needs to be drawn, you will draw it and live by it and swear it really exists objectively and independently of you. But in fact you will be making it up.

Arbitrarily constructed boundaries will fail to describe reality, will fail as a prescription for action, and it will result in suffering. This is why having a practice that guides your action in a healthy way is indispensible and why you have to pick the right group to practice with.

29. Come Together

It is impossible to have a strong practice without a group to practice with. When Sakiyama Roshi decided to completely dedicate his life to Zen meditation he did not just retire into his room. He sought out the company of like-minded people. With them he entered an atmosphere in which practice was encouraged. A place where a practice schedule was maintained, not subject to the whims of an individual, or forced upon anyone.

We need to share our lives. We need the encouragement and support of others. We need to see that our weaknesses are not ours alone, and that we can get stronger as we share our strengths. We need to be challenged and appreciated. And when our fervor for training lags we can enjoy the simple spirit of fellowship and the example of people we admire.

Little by little, instead of a meandering path, our life develops a strong, regular pulse.

Very few people come to our dojo seeking "a life of practice." They just want a few lessons, to learn some moves, to tone up, develop a nice six pack, to feel fearless, or to get focused. Many people first arrive assuming they will train for six weeks or a semester, like the other activities they have done, till they move on to something new.

They think of karate in many ways:

I am 26, I haven't worked out since college and I want to get back in shape before it's too late...

I did Nautilus, I ran, I did machines, and I thought this would be less boring...

I always wanted to do it. I am 17, so it's now or never...

I always wanted to do it. I am 35, so it's now or never...

I always wanted to do it. I am 50, so it's now or never...

I know there is a spiritual aspect to it. Do you do that here?...

I want my kid to get into it...

I want to be more flexible...

I want to feel good...

My cousin does it, in California. He loves it...

I did another style in college, but they don't have that around here...

I want to do some sport with my kids...

I saw a movie about it. It looked pretty cool...

I'm going through a divorce...

On the sign-up card that people fill out when they start there is a box where they can put their reasons for joining and their goals. Most people want to get a good workout and have a good time doing it. Some mention getting self-defense skills. Sometimes people fill out their address and phone number and just stop right there and look at the card and look out the window, and can't tell you what they want.

Sometimes they don't know. Sometimes their reasons are too emotional to admit, to me or even to themselves. Some feel intimidated at work or at school or in some family relationship and they don't want to take it anymore. They sure don't want to write that on a card for a stranger to read. Some feel like they are getting old and want to halt the decline. Some have had a crisis, been attacked or embarrassed.

What we ask of the jocks and the nerds, the men and the women, the adults and the children is in many ways the same. To put on their new white uniform. To stand this way. To walk that way. To bow like this. Don't talk, just copy what you see. And so on. It is simple, it is new, and it is the same for everyone, regardless of their frame of mind or experience. We will explain why to people who want to know why. We approach training this way because it allows everyone to shed their personal habits and limits and act freely. You can set aside your status, high or low, your mood, your abilities, your schedule, everything. And within your capacity, you can simply act.

At first this seems odd to some people. Some people try to bring the skills and status they have in their lives outside the dojo into the dojo, in order to feel more secure as a beginner. For them to let go of that status, maybe for the first time in a long time, especially to become an awkward beginner after years of feeling competent as a parent, a professional, etc., feels strange. But some people find it to be a relief or a thrill. Some people—students, for example—find it pretty much the same as what they do every day anyway.

Each of the people in our dojo is unique. Their abilities and skills and interests vary. But what karate practice asks of each of them is almost identical.

Human beings are always on the lookout for something. We may look poised and satisfied, with a happy, stable life. But until we have completed our training, in the broadest sense, we will be permeated with unease, with wanting, wanting, wanting. And the story will go on and on. People enter the dojo. They bring their karma. We share our lives. A college athlete who wants a challenge she can't get in seasonal sports. An emergency room doctor who gets grief all day from people he patches up. A high school teacher who is trying despite the odds. The father of three who needs to release some stress.

In training we add stress, incrementally, and get so much stronger as a result that often the things we have to deal with outside the dojo seem modest in comparison. Sometimes people feel pressure not from their work but from what their work lacks. They are frustrated. Their jobs are not challenging or rewarding. They feel strapped in and stepped on. They want to devote themselves to something. They want to achieve something. Why not stand tall despite it all? Some people feel good and want to feel even better.

Everyone has a life. There are no 'regular' people.

There is a special class for a group of teenagers who have been involved in violent crime. They are in foster care. Their lives are chaotic. But they like to come to the dojo and learn and workout with a group.

There are classes for children ages 5 to 10. Some parents bring their kids in to watch a children's class, and the kids haven't the faintest interest. Some kids can't wait to start and they talk about it all the time and practice every night at home and can't wait to show their relatives every time they visit. Why is that?

Each of the Moms and Dads and grandmothers and grandfathers, sitting on the benches at the side of the dojo, watching their children in class, has their own story. Each one of the little, unformed five year olds have their own story. Nervous or confident, friendly or sullen, not one of the teenagers in the teen class is a 'type'. If you talk to them you find out that their story is not like anyone else's. Often I don't hear their stories. Usually the members just join in with the rest of the group. Be part of it. Disappear into it. If they are confused or stressed at some point, we help them. If they are struggling, we encourage them. If they are excelling, we praise them. But generally speaking we all just train. Drop the story. Drop the burden of our relentless, human, wish-fulfilling agenda. And just practice.

One woman shyly asked if we would take a deaf child. I said sure. He went to a school for the deaf. He was getting picked on.

She discouraged aggressive behavior but she wanted him to be able to defend himself. She saw an article in a magazine that karate could be good. Up until then she thought it was bad. A neighbor recommended our school. She came and watched.

People showed respect to one another.

It is beautiful to watch, she thought, this is something missing from our lives. For a year from the benches at the side of the room she watched her son's classes. He loved it. Again and again she said she pictured herself in the class. She joined. She had been a painter before her children were born. She did aerobics, went jogging. She had two children 12 years apart. Both unable to hear. Her life became taking care of them, taking them to therapy, loving, praying. "Karate challenges your mind and your body at the same time. You don't have time to worry about anything else." Now she was wearing a white gi, practicing every day and wondering if she could be doing this? "Me?"

Her son asks, "Are you going to keep going until you are a master, Mom?" He says he will keep going until he is a master.

At our dojo everyone who makes effort can succeed. Everyone who has been practicing for a while has an opportunity to teach newer people. Everyone that is new learns from people who are more experienced. Those more experienced people are of all ages, all walks of life, their race or religion known or unknown, becomes irrelevant. All that matters in that time and place is the aspiration to learn and the intention to teach. The social divisions of class, race, age, gender, disappear, leaving no trace.

Does this mean we make no distinctions? Between young and old, male and female, we do make distinctions. Men and women have different body structures so to some degree the physical conditioning varies. Children have a playful atmosphere in their classes with moments of seriousness. Adults are challenged physically and mentally in every class. Older members are not encouraged to do sparring or heavy body contact. People are free to choose their own level of intensity. They get advice, and make their choices. There is no distinction made arbitrarily. Each person gets what they need.

30. The Sopranos

When we watch a compelling story we experience what the characters experience. When we watch a gangster in action we can imagine what it would be like to let our impulses rip. What it might be like if, instead of conducting ourselves with self-restraint, we followed every impulse. What it would be like if we just took what we wanted, lashed out in anger, cracked the heads of anyone who stood in our way, held in contempt all the outsiders, nobodies and losers who minded their manners and suffered in quiet desperation through their dull, regular lives. We may grimace or look away if the movie goes too far. We may rivet our attention to the scene, proving to ourselves and our dates that we're tough enough to deal with the tough reality of life.

However, this isn't 'life' we are witnessing. It's a story. So for the gangster tale to be truly satisfying to an audience of decent people the gangsters have to suffer for what they do. Their violence must be repaid with violence. We want to see that the blanket of contempt they cast over everyone they meet produces in them an uneasy mind full of suspicion and fear. For us to feel good by the end of the movie we must see that these gangsters' cruelty is rewarded with loneliness, misery, and betrayal. Then we have a satisfied feeling.

After mimetically having the fun of running wild, we get to divorce ourselves from the unrestrained, harmful actions of the gangster, and watch in safety, justified in our own life choices. We feel vindicated for having renounced the impulsive, immature, crude, selfish actions of these lowlifes, and instead living morally as a mature, respectful, responsible member of a community, with a happy family and a wholesome life and harmonious relationships with others. But we still watch.

We act out the same kind of fantasies in real life dramas, too. We may in the course of our lives, encounter a charismatic, needy and controlling person who only feels good when they live in a tribe with a clear demarcation separating 'us' and 'them'. We may even go out of our way to meet such a person and join such a group. It can make you feel special. It can make you feel like a 'somebody'.

In the course of our lives we will meet people—they may be annoying or persuasive or charming—who believe that all relationships ought to be turned into relationships of commerce and personal gain. Who believe that it's 'good' somehow to get all your friends and acquaintances to buy your vitamins or your household cleansers even if these 'friends' feel used and so never want to speak to you again. There will be people who believe in their heart that it is not only natural but imperative to turn every human contact into an opportunity to take advantage.

In martial arts the 'organization' only exists as a function of personal relationships, out of friendliness and mutual interest. They are useful only to facilitate the development of the members. Some, however, become corrupt, exploiting the members' need to belong, preying the members naiveté or insecurity . The try to make a cult of a martial arts dojo.

When you begin to practice a martial art you may not have enough knowledge to tell whether or not the art being practiced in that dojo is deep or shallow. But you should be able to tell if the atmosphere is respectful, positive and strong.

I understood that the reason the members of my dojo joined and continued to practice was because they enjoyed it and benefited from it. Some group cultures thrive on feeding an emotional hunger for approval from a manipulative authority figure. Like an unhealthy, abusive personal relationship, dojo cultures can become toxic too. A healthy person will avoid this kind of personal relationship and will avoid it in a martial arts setting too. For martial arts to be relevant in our era teachers have to assure that the art they transmit is deep and practical and also that the human relationships through which it is transmitted are healthy and positive. These are two aspects of a single mission.

31. The Parts of a Person

For most of human history people at all stages of life lived close together. In modern societies we are often segregated by age, status and function. When we do interact with people from a different social segment we do it on the basis of a role—as a professional providing a specific service—instead of as whole people sharing the experience of life. But in the dojo we share our lives naturally.

The kids in the 'juvenile offenders' program, who have their own special class at the dojo, stand out from the other members in their alienation, their rebelliousness and their passivity. They are in the System. Many have been in trouble, in one way or another, since the day they were born. Their lives are chaotic. Sometimes they show up for school, at the classroom next door, carrying everything they own in a paper bag.

The program had been held next door to the dojo for ten years before I ever spoke more than a word or two to anyone there. The kids would stand outside looking away or looking wary or cocky, a few silently eyeballing the karate students and the other people who worked in the building with a practiced affectless gaze.

Then one year a new teacher appeared. She washed the school windows. She decorated the classroom and it looked, for the first time, welcoming.

Each kid has a file that accompanies them to whatever institution they are sent. In the files were logged the facts of their lives, resumes of their contacts with the system. Low birth weight. Mother using drugs and alcohol during pregnancy. Father unknown. Hears voices. Self-mutilation. Drug abuse. In the care of grandmother. In the care of aunt. Homeless shelter. Lived in car. Drug addiction. Gun shot wound at five years old. Stabbing victim. Arrested for violent assault. Arrested for drug possession. Admitted to ER bleeding and incoherent. Signs of multiple personality disorder. Taken from custody of mother. Taken from custody of aunt. And on and on.

The teacher asked if I would do a karate class for them - so they could get some exercise at the end of the day - to help them learn to focus. She would join in too, to help out. She would like to learn it herself. Okay. We can try it. So in they come. Two afternoons a week. Hostile. Suspicious. "I'm not doing it." And why should they? Guys with big pants hanging, felon style, girls in make up, perfume and teen jewelry. They stand at the side of the room by the benches and refuse to move. I look at them. They look at me.

Every Monday when they come back from a chaotic weekend in a new foster home they have a different vibe as if they have taken an emotional pounding. It's bad enough that we cannot hold class for them till Tuesday when they have calmed down and are able to focus on their own lives again.

I ask someone to choke me. I have their attention. I defend against the choke. The one who volunteers to do the choke is one of the more confident and bigger kids, a leader of the group. And when I effortlessly and to his surprise send this big fellow flying across the room, he laughs and the kids think its cool and we all start to have fun. And they begin to enjoy moving and learning. And we get a good workout. And it is like any other class in the dojo after that.

One day we were jumping lightly up and down. I was showing them how to cool down at the end of a workout. One of the kids was jumping really high. Then all the kids started to go really high. So I started to, also. And then I started to jump higher and clap my feet together before falling back down and some of the kids were trying to do it and they were laughing and having a good time for that moment when we heard a snap! Like the sound of a loud hand clap. Or a gunshot. I felt like I was shot in the knee. I stood on one leg, without moving or turning and after a second I regained my composure and conducted the rest of the class just like that, on one foot, without moving.

They asked me if I was okay. I said yeah, and we moved on. I was hurt. They were concerned. That was that. I had to hop down the steps, past them, for the next few days to keep off my swollen knee. Later that week, in our next class, they brought me a pie.

In the corner of the dojo is an oak post, a makiwara, bolted into the floor. It's standard equipment in an Okinawan karate dojo. We punch it to condition our fists. I had told some of the kids that if they hit it hard enough to snap it off they could take it home. One day one guy did it. His hand swelled up like an orange. He hopped around and ran it under water and I assured him it would get better and asked him was it really worth it just to break a piece of already half splintered wood? He assured me that it was, and he was very happy with his prize.

32. A Day's Work

Some people who join our dojo never expected to join. One guy used to bring his kid in on Saturday's. Their Mom brought them during the week, but on the weekends, on Saturday mornings, it was Dad's turn. He's a big guy. The kind you notice as being big, with a chest and forehead like a bull. Like he was bench-pressing mini-vans for his workout. He started out thinking karate was a nice kid-activity. He thought it was good for his boys because they didn't have the means to toughen up as he did when he was a kid.

He grew up on a farm a few miles from where the dojo is now. His family had some of the best farmland in the valley, on the bank of the Connecticut River. Most of the farmers in the valley at that time were recently arrived immigrants, grandparents and great grandparents of the people whose kids are growing up today.

As he tells it, in those days everybody worked, all the time. There was always a job to do and everyone was expected to pitch in. So when he was 10 or 11 years old he did the simple hard repetitive tasks that come with farm life. When he was sent to the barn to cut the tops off of the carrots, this was not, as he puts it, like getting a bunch of them ready for soup. This was a vast heap of carrots, a mountain of them to a ten-year-old, a harvest's worth, which filled the stalls of the barn to overflowing.

He pulled up a stool. Picked up a knife. And started cutting. Throw the tops into an empty stall nearby and the put the cut carrots into another pile. And cut. And throw. Cut. Throw. All day. Till it was done. His whole family worked from morning to night, he says, and they were strong.

When a goat ran off or a stump needed to be pulled from a field, his father just told him to do it. These were considered good jobs for a kid. When he screwed up the penalty was: labor. There was always something to do.

For him, growing up, effort and boredom were always combined, and always present.

He did not want to do this all his life, he said to himself. There's got to be something better to do than farming? This was around the same time that the State took that farm away from his family. It was a successful farm. It provided a livelihood and a home for his family, and had for a generation. But the highway was coming through, Interstate 91 that now runs along the Connecticut River, through Massachusetts from Connecticut to Vermont. The state took the farm. Eminent domain. For the general good. And they didn't pay what it was worth. And this man's family had worked it so hard: it was theirs.

But there was nothing they could do to stop it. The farmers were helpless. The lawyers held all the power. Everything was up to the lawyers. This was about the time when his family told him: You be a lawyer.

How one would go about this he had no idea. But he was determined to do it. So he applied the ethos that had once gotten him through farm work to get through law school. He said it made law school seem pleasant by comparison.

One day he brought his children to the dojo. Growing up in suburban comfort, they didn't have work to do every day. They had activities. And he watched them practice karate, sitting on the bench at the side of the room with the other parents. For some parents it was the only break they would get that day. Some read. Some took off and jogged for 45 minutes. He thought he would like to try karate. It seemed absurd at first. He didn't feel any need for self-defense training. He hadn't met anyone (other than the male members of his own family) he couldn't snap like a dry twig. But there was something great about it. Something familiar and something missing from his life.

It's a different life than the one he grew up in. As a lawyer, the day never ends. You just stop. But the feeling of getting the job done, the satisfaction of having the truck unloaded, the season over, being exhausted, being done for the day, never happens.

In karate it does. You go home exhausted and come back ready. There's a pulse. And you can be tough, as aggressive as you want, and you don't have to go to jail when you're done. And you don't have to make a big deal out of it. No badges, no awards, no nothing. Just the satisfaction of knowing the job, the training period, is done.

A lot of the farm work that a generation ago was done by farm kids today is done by migrant workers. The kids who grew up on those farms, by choice or circumstance, now have no farms to put their effort into. This may explain why half a dozen of the black belt instructors in the school grew up on farms in the Valley.

Physical strength, determination in the face of difficulty and pain, inner stability, are qualities they all have. Those qualities are what they have used to succeed in their own karate practice, what they teach to the other dojo members in their classes, what works in life. It doesn't take values imported from Asia to make practice valuable, successful, or genuine.

Our mental habits, the values we inherit, propel us, even though the form they take may be totally unexpected.

An emergency room can offer an opportunity to help people in crisis. It can also seem like drudgery or a siege. The river of suffering is never-ending. But for some ER doctors, like anyone who is obliged to help each day, their own pain can from time to time eclipse that of the people who come to them in need.

That this is a function of mind not outer circumstance is not obvious. Tell a high school teacher with an out of control class, or a heartbroken lover, that their suffering is a function of their state of mind and, in the midst of difficulty, it will be too hard for them to grasp. If they do nothing, they will probably keep suffering. However, if they take action, in the right way, they will start to see some light.

A member of the dojo sees 40 patients a day in the emergency room of a city hospital. A few he can help. Many people who come to his emergency room come not because they are facing a life-threatening emergency but because they are upset. Almost every day some woman arrives by ambulance having faked a fainting spell during a fight with a boyfriend. People come in with constipation and demand a CAT scan. People come in sad or frustrated or lonely and make hysterical demands. Knowing that this is a symptom of their helplessness does not make it any easier for him to deal with. Because people curse at him when he refuses unnecessary treatments or tests it became a personal struggle. His level of anxiety became intolerable.

After years of this, conflict became his mode of operation not just with patients, but with staff and administrators. Everyone wanted something from him, but few seemed to appreciate what he was doing for them or their families.

He joined the dojo. He was angry. It showed in his kata. Because each person is practicing the same sequence of movements it is easy to spot the subtle variations that reveal the inner life of each person. If someone is lax or tense, impulsive or shy, aggressive or timid, guarded or open, phony or honest, happy or sad, lazy, courageous, angry or greedy it will be immediately visible in their kata.

If they persevere the kata will have a tonic effect on their body and emotions, an effect that goes deeper and deeper the longer we practice.

This ER doctor trained hard at the dojo every day. The pressure to move well, to meet the demands of training, demands made by your body, your instructor, your opponent or training partners, changes you. Your own effort to learn what to do and to do it well—to gain speed, strength and skill, and to eliminate the gap between your intention and your action—makes you stronger and humbler at once.

What's there to prove, if you've really got the goods? Nothing. You can relax. You won't hold excess tension in your body after a hard workout. The tension drops away. And the relaxation that naturally results feels good.

He experienced this. He returns to the dojo day after day and works out hard again. That pulse begins to regulate his body and mind so now he can relax, and push hard, and relax again.

What impressed him, even before he had learned much karate, was that in the dojo you are working with people who are all trying to do their best. That came as a relief. Although each person, individually, may be strong or weak, a great athlete or a desk jockey, as a group they were all moving forward, focused not on aches and pains and obstacles, but on being free of them. In the dojo he had found people who realized that aches and pains were part of daily life. People who respected each other and themselves. Who did not presume that someone else ought to do things for them, but who were willing to do for themselves and for others, any time. The restraint the senior members showed in placing demands on the newer members made it possible for each person to learn easily and help generously where it was really needed. No one in need was ignored. No one presumed upon the generosity of the stronger individuals.

Here was a model he could apply to the emergency room. Even if he could not change his working environment, he found a way to change the way he dealt with it. And he had the composure he needed to implement the model. Be cool. Be rational. Be respectful. Talk to people. See where they are coming from.

Now when the man who slashes his abdomen open once every month or so and stuffs things like lifesavers, utensils, tools, and pamphlets into the wound, comes in to the emergency room for treatment, he just takes care of the guy as best he can.

When he wades into the river of suffering that never stops, suffering that appears to be self-inflicted, which once appeared to be an assault on society, a waste and abuse of the hospital's resources, now appears differently to him. When people arrive in pain or crazy, begging for a witness to their misery and confusion, he does what he can do.

33. What's Going On

Growing up, when I saw a street full of people, buses, trains full, streets jammed with traffic, car after car after car flying down the highway, each person intent on their own private urgent objective, I often wondered

"What are they all doing?"

Walking in the mountains in a thick fog, high up and far from everywhere. I had been walking up there for days. The weather was cold and getting colder, and the moisture in the air soaked me to the skin in minutes. I was flying along the trail. This was the one place where I felt I fit perfectly. I was like everything I could see, and it was like me.

On a steep narrow rock-covered section of trail I walked pressed against a cliff that towered over me and disappeared up into the mist. Water collected on the rock and seeped down. It poured down in little freshets. I stepped easily from stone to stone around the streams and ascended through the thickening fog.

I saw people coming toward me once or twice. They smelled like soap, and their faces looked grim. They weren't having fun anymore. They had blisters on their feet. This was a section where you really had to pay attention, it wasn't soaring and exhilarating like the experience they had planned on when they started out, which, I could tell from the smell of them, was no earlier than yesterday.

As I got up to the ridge, a mile above the surrounding landscape, the trail flattened out. Here you didn't have to pay such close attention to the ground. You could look out and see forever. See the rivers glittering, the dark folds of the valleys, the peaks of all the other mountains receding into the blue distance. You could see everything. You could see a little car going along on a twisting line of road. You could hear a plane engine, or something man-made, far off. You could walk fast.

Except now the fog was moving in so thick I could hardly see my boots. I could vaguely see the edges of the trail. But I could only follow it by looking straight down. Without realizing it, I began to fall. Falling forward with every step. Landing with a shock on my forward foot, again and again and again. Slipping now and then between damp granite cobbles.

I couldn't tell if I was going slow or fast. I couldn't tell if I was going right. There was supposed to be a shelter ahead but how far? I knew the route, but no markers had been visible for a long time. The wind blew thick patches of fog completely whiting out the trail. Even the trees a foot or two away vanished in it. Then for a second the air would clear and I could get a glimpse of the scene fifty or sixty feet ahead, to the next marker or the next cross, marking the spot where someone died, and then on further, to the white nothing.

I was like a robot. Banging out steps. But I was stumbling from time to time. My feet felt like mush in my boots and I couldn't tell quite where the ground was supposed to be. It seemed further down than I expected. I wasn't tired. Although I could not feel it, I was freezing. I trudged on and walked directly into the side of the shelter, which had been completely whited out by the clouds. It hit me in the chest as if I was just standing there and a building came up at three miles an hour and slammed into me. I pulled open the door. There was someone there. I tried to speak but could not.

But I got there.

Stumbling along, unsure of the path, I proceeded.

I used a similar process, stumbling along unsure of the path, to answer "What is everyone doing?" I asked the question, to myself, as young as I can remember. When my world was bounded by the subway that ran next to the kitchen window of our apartment in the Bronx, shaking the room when it went by every five minutes.

The world was concrete, carpet, linoleum, marble, vacant lots filled with debris to play in, and at night the sound of dogs and the smell of fire. Somewhere out there, I could see in the distance, there was another world illuminated by stadium light towers, lights blazing blue-white in the night.

The question just rested in my mind, and for a long time I didn't have a clue as how to answer it. But I would look down from the window. Down the street to the bus stop, and out to the endlessly rushing river of cars on the highway heading over the bridge to New York or out away from the city, all those people in cars, in suits, with briefcases and newspapers, faces looking humorless and determined, clearly doing something, something important to them, but what? Why was it important? Why was I not in that state too? What did their world have to do with me?

I questioned adults about God. About the big picture, about the way life worked, what the structure of life is, the rules of human relationships and the relationship of people to God. About what God actually wanted from people, and about what people could expect from God. I made up answers, wild and tame, and tried them out on adults. The reactions ranged from amusement to perplexity to scorn but I was sure I was on the right track. What I wanted to know was, "What is worth doing? We have one life, I don't want to waste it. I want to dedicate it totally to ...what exactly?"

I did not know. I could not get an answer. I did not know anyone who was doing something like what I had in mind. And what I had in mind was indistinct, a feeling, not a picture, and it wasn't a feeling I could name. I wavered between searching for an unknown objective on the one hand, and on the other wanting to drop the whole business and join the flow of life I felt around me.

What was similar between that walk in the mountains and the way I went about answering that question was that both were characterized by an unquestioned determination to go forward, insufficient knowledge to proceed safely, and the fact that the object of my search seemed to just appear, to materialize fully-formed, on its own.

34. A Dojo

I was about 20, in the 1970s, living on a back road in a 1790s farmhouse with some friends. Every once in a while, on a Saturday afternoon, a pale face would appear at the window. It was a guy who lived way out in the woods, in a little cabin. He wanted to be totally self-sufficient. His face was expressionless. His traveling buddies were a long hunting knife and a bottle of Jack Daniel's. He would say: "Hey, I don't like people much." I thought he added the "much" as a loophole to permit his visit, what with us being people and all. He'd say, "I like it on my own."

He lived in the woods. He built his own house, grew a garden, hunted and fished for food. He built his furniture and cut his wood.

He only went to town, he said, for tobacco and gasoline. Uh huh. But he seemed to always stop by our house on the way. Always with a reason: to borrow a tool, or to drop off some vegetables. He wouldn't say "for company," but if he had it would have been acceptable. That's a necessity too.

Zen monks in Korea live together in a monastery setting for a few months or a year and then move on. They move on to another monastery, individually or in small groups. There they practice with a new group of monks—some familiar, some strangers. At each new place they study from a fresh perspective under a different Zen teacher.

In each place they follow the familiar rules that organize and govern monastery life. So even though they are in a location that is new, the mores and customs are familiar. Even when surrounded by strangers they can feel at home. They know how to conduct themselves, when to be where, which relationships are relationships of obligation and which are merely polite.

Some monks want to live in solitary retreat, as hermits. That is not a lifestyle choice. It is a practice method, and it is temporary. Generally they live alone for about six months and then return to community life inside the monastery walls.

Groups support us and we support them. It feels good. TV and air conditioning will not substitute for human relationships any more than drugs and alcohol will. We need our family. Community. Congregation. Team. Club. Company. Country. Through them we define ourselves. We have a purpose. We share a purpose. Our efforts yield results. We are appreciated. We reflect the lives of others. We are loved. We can work hard and we can rest.

Groups vary in character and they change in character over time. Like individuals. When we are in a group, or are considering joining one, we consciously or unconsciously consider:

What motivation do the people in this group have for being part of the group? What are they doing? What actions are they asking me to take? What will taking the action mean? What will be the result of my actions?

We may also ask: What constitutes this group?

If we assume the group exists on its own, with its energy received by its members and not generated by its members, then its energy will wind down. It will not serve the interests of the members. Like the two old guys in the basement bar of the fraternal organization that was jam-packed forty years ago but today is just them, the President and the Chairman. For those guys it may just be a little sad. When it happens to companies, to political parties, to countries, to dojos, it can be dangerous.

When this decline happens people will cling to the memory of what the group once was, then concoct a fictional set of characteristics that they pretend that membership in the group confers on them. This fiction will, over time, diverge further and further from reality: whereas once the members had a sense of shared purpose, current members are occupied more and more by empty rituals and titles, harking back to the glory days. This is why some people are bored with their church or temple, political party, civic group or dojo while the members from an earlier time still get a charge out of it. The juice that got it going has drained away, living only in the memory of people who were a part of it long ago.

A well-run group, like a well-lived life, generates energy. A poorly run one dissipates energy. This is because groups do not have any fixed characteristics of their own, but rather depend on the actions of the members. The actions of the members can be measured on two axes: virtuous/non-virtuous and active/passive.

That's why when I opened my dojo I needed to answer: What is a *dojo*?

A room? No it can't be a room because the room our dojo is in once housed a factory filled with rows of five-ton forges that pounded sheets of metal into knives and forks and spoons, for a hundred and fifty years before we got there. And when we move out someone else will move right in. Several times a year we travel to practice at a beach or a lake or in the woods. We say "the dojo is going to the beach this weekend…" The dojo isn't the room.

Is the dojo the group of people? Not really, because since we opened thousands of people have come and gone. And although some of the current members have been practicing consistently for a long time none of them were there the first day we opened, except

me. None of them have been there every day, and none will be
there some years in the future, including me, and yet it still is and
will be "the dojo."

Does a dojo consist of a style of movement, a particular
knowledge set? Is it a certain way of moving or a group of
techniques taught via a teaching lineage? There are many places
that teach the kind of techniques we teach, but they are not all our
dojo. And if you compared the way I moved the day I opened to the
way we move now, you would see that the quality of the practice
has changed and deepened. We teach many techniques with a very
different understanding than we once had. We teach ways of moving
that we didn't know then. We have added some valuable insights and
have discarded some methods that were not good.

The teaching lineage itself is not a particular thing. It is not
a precisely defined chain of people who passed on an unaltered
system from generation to generation. The lineage has had many
influences. Many cultures crossed paths on Okinawa. For at least
500 years many transmission streams, flowing from different regions
of China, from all over South Asia and beyond, were filtered by
generations of Okinawan teachers and often mixed with their own
indigenous fighting methods.

Selections—what the Okinawans and their teachers learned
and what they passed on—were made based on the aptitudes
and understandings, prejudices, compromises and discoveries of
the practitioners. Additions and deletions were made over time.
Continually. Intentionally and unintentionally. Styles are fluid. They
are not stable, not fixed at some point in history. We can document

that martial arts styles are not found artifacts. They are alive and responsive to conditions. The dojo is not the "style."

Is the dojo me? No. I am not there all the time. I teach only a fraction of the classes on the schedule each week. The dojo would still exist if I were gone tomorrow.

So what is it? We know it exists. We know it exists because we have been practicing. Our bodies and minds and lives have changed. We have experienced this. We know it. It's having a real effect on our lives. But what is it, exactly?

Is this an important question? Answering it correctly provides an excellent antidote for the mistaken assumption that the dojo is an institution with fixed qualities. That it is some thing that can and will exist independent of the lives of all the people who practice in it.

We tend to take for granted the objective existence of the things that sustain us. Then, sometimes, we presume upon them or take unfair advantage of them. By cashing in the investment of spiritual capital (honest hard work, for example) that earlier members made in the group, we damage what was sustaining us. For example, crooks who rig financial markets depend for the success of their crime on the trust that their predecessors built, through their honest dealing. The same kind of corruption can happen in a dojo when people wear ranks they do not honor with hard work and good conduct, but instead trade on their predecessors' reputation. This deception hurts their group in the future, the other members, and ultimately will ruin their own chances of happiness. It is similar to the way in which people sometimes take their families or their marriages for granted. For example they may operate in the false assumption that their job is theirs for good. Or make the same false presumption as the old European nobility who thought their social position, income, and relationships were fixed and based on qualities inherent in them. Sometimes people take their spiritual life as something bestowed and guaranteed; as if nothing were required of them to make their inner life sound.

When we act as if the world will retain its shape regardless of our action then decline will result. When we recognize the impermanence of all aspects of our lives we can begin to see that our happiness depends exclusively on doing right.

35. The Crucible of Karma

A dojo is a collection of karma—human actions and
accumulated mental habits—that we label as a dojo. Since a dojo
is made only of actions, it follows that if you want to create a good
dojo you need to do what's right.

Our lives are made of actions. Answering the question of what
to do and what to avoid is essential. This question, expressed in a
primitive way, was what I was asking when I wondered again and
again, "What are they all doing?"

In the Abhidharma, an ancient collection of Buddhist doctrine,
there is a description of the cosmos. It is fundamental to an
understanding of Indian Buddhism but it is generally ignored by
contemporary Buddhists. Abhidharma cosmology seems to be a
relic of pre-scientific, ignorant times. It seems to be mistaken, a
flaw, irrelevant. It is regarded as the Asian facsimile of Ptolemy
or the Flat Earth Society. Something you might study if you were
interested in the history of science, but not a place to look for truth.

This misses the point. As an analog of our inner geography it's
as precise as an atomic clock.

The Abhidharma describes a vast ocean from which four
continents arise. These four continents are arranged around the base
of a huge central mountain, Mount Meru. Humans live on one of
the continents, the continent called "Endurance." If a person were to
travel in any direction away from Mount Meru, he would eventually
encounter a range of iron mountains. It would be impossible to walk

around the mountain range, because the range is a circle completely surrounding Mount Meru. If, with great effort and determination the person climbed up and over the iron mountain range he could keep going for a while, but before too long he would encounter another ring of mountains. Struggle on? There's another and another, seven of them, until, if he chose to persevere despite the difficulty, he will arrive at the nothing at the edge of the world.

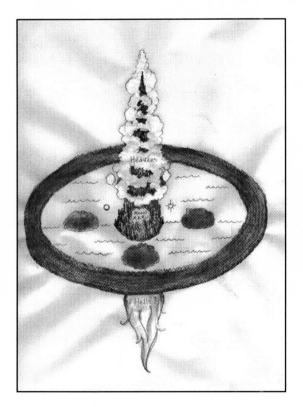

So let's say our traveler has discovered that heading away from the center of the world, no matter how far he goes, will yield only exhaustion. If this person, seeing the futility of his earlier efforts was still inclined to travel, he could only head inward, toward the central axis of the world.

There, he could go up or down. Going up a mountain takes effort; more effort than staying in place. And going up the central mountain takes more energy than climbing the rings of iron mountain ranges, because it is much taller. But this ascent is worth the work. There, through the clouds, are the heavens. Thirty-three of them, each one more joyous and more glorious than the last, populated by gods and angels and other heavenly beings. And up beyond them are the Buddha realms, paradises completely beyond suffering.

What if the traveler instead of ascending, heads downward? Going down is easy. It takes passivity, or stupidity, not energy or intelligence. If we expend our life energy in thrall of our impulses, or in hot pursuit of poisonous things, we descend further and faster.

On the surface of the world, the human and animal realms mingle. Down below Mount Meru on the central axis of the world are the lower realms. Below, if we descend, we come first to the realm of the hungry ghosts. They spend their lives there desperate for food and drink. They are in constant agony and desperately search everywhere, but they rarely find anything that will satisfy them. If they do they find something to eat or drink they suffer more because their mouths are too small to sip and their throats are too small to swallow. Sometimes, when they find water to quench their thirst, it burns their lips like fire. Sometimes they see what looks like a fresh, cool stream, but as they approach it transforms into a river of blood and pus.

Further down below Mount Meru are the hells. Eight hot hells, eight cold hells. The suffering of beings in hell starts as horrific, and should they descend to the lower hells, gets unimaginably worse.

The scriptural descriptions of these realms are elaborate. Nevertheless an overall theme is implicit. Mere expenditure of energy is not enough to have a good life. In fact, by moving away from the central axis, we expend our lives fruitlessly. This represents a path of relentless accumulation. It leads nowhere. No matter how much wealth, fame, information, worldly power one accumulates, where does it lead? Sought for its own sake, what does it come to?

This cosmological metaphor captures accurately the futility of the attempt to master the universe through the accumulation of scriptural knowledge, scientific knowledge, pleasurable sense experiences, philosophy, etc. All these worldly goals hold out the promise of happiness, providing us with temporary satisfactions, but leaving us in the end without a lasting source of happiness. We exhaust ourselves, exhaust our lives, and never achieve our aim. Our goals recede endlessly, while new ones appear, again and again as the next ring of iron mountains, far in the distance.

This represents the mental habit of always wanting, and so, always wanting more. It describes the futility of seeking happiness out there, somewhere where it will never be found, no matter how intrepid our search.

What will actually make a difference in the quality of our lives is the moral valence of our action. If we behave virtuously we ascend. If we behave non-virtuously, we descend. Whether you are a banker, teacher, doll collector, supermodel or mail carrier, you have a choice every moment as to whether your mental condition and your actions are virtuous, non-virtuous or neutral. You can waste your life, condemn yourself to suffer, or free yourself from suffering forever.

You do not have to apprehend the subtleties of Zen stories to gain this view or to walk this path. Anyone, in any religion, in any walk of life, can do it.

Whether or not you take these specific cosmological descriptions to represent actual locations in space and time is not the point here. The metaphor as a guideline for action here and now, is accurate.

Whether you are an artist, a scientist, teacher, a parent or anything else, the implication of this teaching is not to suggest that you abandon your pursuit. But rather to be sure that you are motivated by a desire to put an end to suffering for all beings, and that you work as hard and skillfully as you can to realize that motivation.

According to this cosmology what determines your ascent or descent are your actions and mental habits, i.e., your karma. Birth in some of the heavens, for example, is the result of habitually experiencing the pleasure of certain meditative mental states in this life. Birth in others is the result of profound and continual kindness. Other, higher heavens are the destination for individuals who dedicated their lives to achieving the deepest states of peace and understanding.

A future as a hungry ghost is the natural and unavoidable outcome of greed, hoarding, constantly wanting, depriving others of what they need while you have plenty. Eons in the hells are the destiny of those who killed and committed other terrible crimes, who did so repeatedly, thought of it as good, and wanted to do it some more.

It is possible to study the means by which karma works—how all the things we do, say and think plant seeds in our minds, and how these seeds germinate and have their effects on us later. But even without understanding the intricate mechanics of karma, we can get useful guidance from this cosmological description of what is good to do and what is harmful. If we take it to heart, we can live a worthy life.

I reflected on the implications of this with regard to building a dojo. It is not enough to expend energy. When I was starting the dojo the image of an old-time gold prospector crossed my mind. Some guy who spent his whole life baking and digging in the desert, at first enthusiastically looking for the Mother Lode, then just looking for a river to pan, then hoping for a nugget, then just being an old guy in the desert. Enthusiasm in the quest is not enough to assure success.

Dozens of dojos have come and gone in our town in the years since we opened ours. Some opened with fanfare, ad campaigns, give-aways, direct mail pitches and video news releases. Some fizzled out, disappearing over night, some did bake sales and car washes for a while before they closed. Some signed up their students to three-year contracts and then ran off to another state with the money. They all start with energy, imagining they will do well. But something derails them. It is not something in society, in the system, in the character of "people nowadays." If that were the case then our dojo wouldn't have worked either. What derails them is something in their own actions—what they do, say, or think.

Staying focused on gain, or staying in the additive phase of practice for too long, is like slogging ever onward toward the rings of iron mountains. No matter how many styles you have studied, how many techniques you know, how much theoretical understanding you amass, you will not get to the end of it. As the returns on energy expended in accumulation diminishes, you burn out.

Corporations feel the continual pressure to grow larger. Children have to grow larger, too. As mature practitioners we undermine the quality of our lives and the effectiveness of our practice if we are only focused on getting more and getting bigger. As adults we need depth and subtlety, not just "growth". Making our choices properly will determine whether we ascend, or just waste our chance.

We have only a few decades to practice. It's our brief opportunity for freedom. We have to practice with the right motivation, use the right means, and to examine, every step of the way, the results. Otherwise we risk wasting our lives running around the desert. Or, if we habitually engage in non-virtuous action and spread negative mental states through our school, encouraging states of mind such as hatred, rage, greed, inclination toward the use of intoxicants, sexual misconduct, gossiping, criticizing others and so on, the bad results will multiply.

There is no such thing as generic "martial arts". A woman in her fifties asked me if she should keep doing karate. Is she too old, she asked? I asked her: What do you want from it? She said she didn't know. I told her, once you know what you want you can use karate to get it. What karate is to you depends on you.

Another guy was getting ready for boot camp. He wanted to stay at the dojo for hours after class, pounding the targets and hitting the heavy bag, practicing furiously into the night. I gave him a key.

36. The Alchemy of Action

Genuine martial arts training is a kind of alchemy. We work in a laboratory where the crude stuff of our body and mind are transmuted into something exquisitely rare, refined and complete.

In the words Oku Myo Zai Ren Shin embroidered on our black belts, the word Ren connotes "forging", as in making steel.

You have to know how to make the process work, but it is not essential to start out with a theoretical understanding. You just have to practice.

As I began training it was a matter of just pushing my body and mind beyond their limits. I read that this promised a kind of purification. That was enormously appealing. Realization and liberation, I was given to understand, would naturally follow.

The heat and pressure of transformation comes from the carefully calibrated pressure you put on your own body and mind and from your willingness to learn from your unpredictable interactions with others.

37. The Old Mill

From time to time I get a letter or a postcard from a former dojo member with a photo of the Thames or the Spanish Steps, from Ghana, Puerto Rico, Madison, Dusseldorf or Milwaukee. People say: I am here and I am looking for a place to practice. Some of the people who have sent those postcards have returned to our dojo, five or ten years later. Some start again, the second time around with their kids. There have been many people who tried it who didn't like it, people who loved it then didn't, people who drifted in and drifted out. But I hear from time to time that they still think about it.

Our dojo is one room, a forty foot square, with benches on one side. There is a small office, changing rooms for the men and women, and a hall to the bathrooms and the shower. The walls are old, orange brick, with 8-foot high windows along two walls. The ceilings are 12 feet high. The floor is wood.

We're on the second floor of an old mill, overlooking a bend in the Mill River, in Northampton, Massachusetts. This mill is one of hundreds that were built along the rivers up here during the 19th century, the water power running the factories was the fountain of success for the industrial pioneers of the time.

Looking down from my office window I see the gravel parking lot sloping slightly away from the building, and at the far edge a row of heavy stones lined up along the steep high bank to keep cars from sliding over into the river on icy winter nights (they have done their job many times). Thirty feet below the stream bounces through the

boulders in the summer and fall, freezes over in the winter, and in the spring is a roaring torrent.

If you look closely, there in the bottom of the stream you can see discarded fragments of cutlery, mistakes and scraps the metal workers tossed down there. People threw everything into the stream, and into the old canal that used to run where our parking lot is now. Once a tie rod appeared through the gravel in the middle of the parking lot. People pulled at it once in a while as they walked by, like it was Excalibur. After a while a bucket-loader came and yanked at it and up came the whole front end of a car. Somebody probably pushed it into the old canal in the 30s, the driver said.

The knives, forks and spoons, stamped in the forges that once pounded away in the space we now occupy provided a living for generations of people growing up in this neighborhood. The mill was still running when I first checked it out as a place to put the dojo. By then, the 1980s, the mill's technology was out of date, the business was failing, and real estate prices were rising.

A few of the forges were still in place the winter before we moved in. The men working at them stood in their overcoats while they worked, wearing gloves, not just because the metal was still hot when it came out of the machines, but because when it was 15 degrees outside it was 25 degrees inside. Snow drifted down through holes in the roof. Through the worn and weathered wide pine plank floors you could see people working downstairs, on the floor below. They were not mill workers working down there that winter. They were builders. Figuring what it would take to renovate the building, to attract new tenants and make the place profitable again.

A full circle was closed when we moved in. It was Chinese influence that got the place built in the mid nineteenth century. It was Chinese influence bringing it to life again, a century and a half later, when we moved in.

The building went up in the 1840s, when Abraham Lincoln was still splitting rails and steam ship travel was news. By that time the Industrial Revolution had been underway in England for nearly a century. Tens of thousands of people streamed in to the big cities of

England, to escape the poverty and monotony of rural life. Factory work in the cities held the promise, if not of happiness, at least of less unhappiness. The people worked, mostly by hand, in factories. Sanitation was poor. Water in the cities was usually polluted, so people drank wine instead. This was a problem for employers, since the workers were half-drunk by midday. It was especially bad when the weather was hot and people were thirsty.

The solution came by way of China, in the form of the new drink, "tea". Tea became wildly popular. It elevated people's mood. Employers noticed that it made workers work harder. They were more efficient and more energetic after a cup of tea. Caffeine was not given the credit immediately, but it worked.

Tea became stylish. And the addiction to it was cultural as well as biochemical. Enthusiasm for tea coincided with the rise of the newly affluent working and middle class in England. These people had money to spend and social aspirations to fulfill. One of the ways in which they did both was through domestic table service, *de rigueur* for the well-appointed home: imported porcelain tea sets ("china") for serving and drinking tea, accompanied by appropriate utensils on the table for refined eating, in the style of aristocrats.

Demand for tableware was growing too fast for English manufacturers to supply. The rivers around Northampton, England were saturated with mills. But in America land was cheap and labor was plentiful. New England was laced with a dense network of waterways. The profit was there to be made. The first section of our building was built in 1840. Other sections were added over the years, as the business prospered.

A woman who grew up in our neighborhood, and moved away to go to college, loved hearing the sound of the Cutlery Mill, the pounding of the forges at night, as she went off to sleep. As a child it was comforting to her. She said it sounded like all the world was in its place, and all was well.

Now, time (in the form of us) has replaced the sounds of those forges with the sounds of kiai's echoing through the neighborhood. It was not a welcome sound to some of the neighbors, at first. But now everyone is acquainted with us and how we sound. Now we are as familiar as the sound of the forges once were.

38. Innocence & Experience

The formality with which we conduct our classes is a tool. It provides continuity amid change. It provides an efficient way to convey technique, without the distraction of premature analysis, self-consciousness, or personal considerations. It is a good way to train for a crisis. High-pressure situations may provoke all sorts of emotions. If we get stuck on feelings we will not have the clarity to act. That is why we learn to not show any expression during training. The formality and silence of training appealed to me all along. But I was not very good at explaining it at first.

Years ago a guy asked one of the other students, indignantly, why he had to sweep the floor at the end of class, when he paid good money to come here. No one asks that kind of question any more. Because no one feels like a peon. It is clear, now, that the dojo belongs to all of us. So now it's natural that everyone pitches in. We are all in it together. We all feel that way. So now sweeping the floor is not onerous. It is one of many ways in which we take care of ourselves, our place, and each other.

When I quit going to the Zen center in the Catskills I told the head man that I was going to stop coming there. He told me well, we hate to lose students, but....

We had that conversation about a year after I opened my karate dojo, and it opened my eyes: It is foolish for leaders of groups to think they "have" students or members. I had no special connection to that man. He had never spoken to me personally. He did not "have" me as a student. But it's easy for leaders of groups to make that presumption.

I never again thought that I "had" a student. I was careful to remember that what I had was a relationship with a person. If the relationship was respectful and mutually beneficial it would continue. If it was not, it would end.

I did have some understanding of the methods of training. But I lacked the human warmth that would have put my concern for the individual student in that specific place and time ahead of my commitment to a method, or my own ideal conception of how a dojo should be.

I discovered I had to run a place that people would love to come to, not just a place that was authentic and intense. A psychologist who joined my dojo in the first few months after I opened, stood under a cascading hot shower after a class and called out to me: "It's aversive, it's aversive!" God knows what the rest of them were thinking in those first days.

39. The Thrills of Purgatory

The dojo began as an empty room, with me, sleeping on the floor at night, practicing kata and putting up the walls during the day. After a while I hung a sign outside the door announcing karate lessons. I named the place. I made a schedule. One at a time, people came to check it out. Now hundreds of people come each week to train. Someday the room will again be empty. Someone else will come in and decide it just might work for them, and they will launch their imagination into reality, right here. Like the cutlery makers did. Like I did. But now, in the heat of the life of the dojo, there's alchemy underway every day.

At our dojo people usually practice about three times a week. Three times a week they take time out of their schedules. They take a few hours away from their family, their jobs, from schoolwork. Some bring their family and all take class together. Some drag themselves away from their friends, some finish their homework early, some get to it later. Some use their lunchtime. Some put an employee in charge of the shop and take off for an hour or two.

You pull into the parking lot and you shut off your car and you pick up your bag with your uniform in it. You walk along the edge of the lot next to the river and you can hear it and smell it, and as you veer away across the parking lot toward the building the sound of the river fades. You go up the steps to the balcony that runs along the building on the second floor. As you get to the top you can hear the river roar again. You put your shoes in the rack outside the door and go in.

The sequence is the same for every person but the event is
never the same twice. One guy just flies up the stairs can't wait to
break out of the straightjacket of his day job. One trudges dutifully,
wishing he was home in front of the TV but telling himself that
when he is done he will feel better and he will have earned his
eggplant. One woman's face looks drawn and determined, having
just broken up with her boyfriend, she's changed jobs and she's
moving this week, but at least she has this one thread in her life to
hold onto. Two boys start to make the transition from teenagers
getting out of Mom's van into young men about to undergo a test
of courage. Two women talk, smiling easily, without a hint of what
they are about to do. One guy just closed the biggest deal of his life.
One dropped a hammer through a window he was hanging. One
lady just got through a horrific therapy session, sure she will never
be the same (and she is the therapist). One comes hoping to see her
one true love, as she usually does in this class. Another hopes she
won't see her former boss. Everyone brings their own story. And
once they cross the threshold, they drop it. There are times when
thoughts intrude. What you have to do tonight. What you should
have said to that jerk at work today. How great life is. How miserable
you are. How you miss someone. You practice setting it aside. You
follow the form of the class. You train.

Every move and every moment in the class is part of the form.
You bow when you enter. You sign in. You change into your
uniform. You greet another student with a bow. None of this is
done in a stiff, unnatural way. People say hello and so on. But it
has a form. You begin practice with a partner before class starts. A
senior will approach a newer student or a new student will approach
a more advanced one and as they partner up they bow and greet

each other with the polite Japanese expression "Onegaishimasu," meaning "I ask something of you." Then they practice a technique or form that the newer person is learning.

When two senior people are practicing together the vibe is different. It sometimes is just fun. They will share their discoveries about the application of a move in a kata they are practicing, or an insight into a technique they never understood before: "Look at the way this move works, hey watch what happens when you step like this and strike here, or try pushing like this, or look how could this work, use the back of the wrist..." Then someone goes flying, a technique snaps instantly into place, and the mood shifts to serious, challenging, fast and aggressive.

The laughs and smiles dissolve and sweat begins to bead up on their faces. They radiate energy and sometimes the newer people find it hard not to stop what they are doing and just watch those guys. In a minute or two the seniors stop. They try the move a second time, a third, a fourth. Discovering the elegance in a technique that before seemed obscure or too crude to work.

Then class begins. Silence. People line up in ranks, with the most senior in the front. We bow. We do a warm up exercise sequence, the same sequence at the start of every class. During the class there is focused practice from beginning to end.

We practice this way because it produces good results, most quickly. The demands of the form require us all to drop our personal psychological preoccupations. No one can keep their attention on those preoccupations and meet the demands of each moment of the class at the same time. After class, when those concerns return to the students' awareness, they do not seem to loom quite as large as they did, just an hour or two before. So ironically, by following this precisely prescribed form, we experience freedom.

The other day I saw a kid walking around on Main Street, in Northampton. He took classes at our dojo when he was about 7. Now he is 13. He was sitting on the corner half-heartedly begging for money from passersby. He is in the ninth grade. His parents work. The kids he grew up with are doing sports, homework and hanging out around town while this kid spends his afternoons pretending to be an addict. He got caught shoplifting. I said, "What are you doing?" He looks at me like he doesn't know what I'm talking about. Then focus comes to his eyes. He smiles in a sly way. "This is reality." To him it is. To his parents, to his grandparents, his brother, his neighbors, it isn't. In fact to them the life he is living is distinctly unreal, it is nothing but a pretense.

A few days later my wife and I were walking by a river. At a place where the water was completely still, clear enough so I could see the stones on the bottom without any distortion. There were colored leaves falling that day, floating on the surface of the water here and there. The light glinting on the surface of the water, igniting the leaves, illuminating the riverbed, seemed breathtakingly still and clear. It didn't appear to me as just an aesthetic perfection. It seemed to exist with an intensity of reality distinct from that of the world I ordinarily experience.

Like some of the intense training experiences I had, that moment had a feeling of exaltation, release, of correctness, and of overwhelming stillness. That sense of reality does not exist simply in the objects we perceive. It is a mirror of the condition of the mind. I had looked at the river at that spot a hundred times and it never looked the way it looked that day. The appearance of that river at that moment was my perception of the river through my karma, the mental habits and structure that were ripening and which then composed my mind. All our experiences are formed in this way.

When I first started training, looking back I can see we were not so much learning a practice as learning an attitude. It was a smug, tribal attitude, with a swagger to it. It felt good. But it's not good for you. There was a price. There was always a worry about who was loyal and who was drifting away, which rival dojos or martial arts styles were a threat and which would crumble. The emphasis on making a tight "in-group" was energizing and harmful, like a drug, because it served as a substitute for doing deep practice or exploring real technique. We were convinced that was "real." It was invigorating, but it made the world around us appear shadowy.

40. Initiation

Kids need a challenge to grow. If you don't give them one they will find one on their own.

Sometimes children come into the dojo wild. They jump around and make faces at themselves in the mirror. Sometimes they come in tamed. Drugged with Ritalin, compliant and slack. Most of them start shy, excited and happy to be there.

One young single mom told me that although she never gave her son toy guns or anything like that to play with, and never let him see action videos, one day he just started picking up sticks and swinging them. Dueling! Jumping off fences and rocks, battling imaginary enemies across the backyard.

This behavior confused her. Boys play like that. If you direct that play you can get good results: they can develop physical skill, focus and self-control. And they learn to equate strength with the ability to help and protect, not the power to do harm. That is how a positive dojo culture channels wild energy. Without that channeling the energy will still be present, but it will deform.

When the children first walk in to the dojo they pair off with a partner or two. The more experienced ones show the newer ones what to do.

Then, when the instructor calls the start of class, the children stop what they're doing, bow, and line up. We kneel together and sit silently for a minute, settling down. Then everyone jumps to their

feet, and we move in unison, warming up. Some of the kids are
spacey and wiggly, and some of the newer ones have a hard time
telling right from left or what to do next but they pick up on it and
no one criticizes them. They start to get what is going on and soon
they learn it well. We like them. They know it. We ask a lot of them.
They want to accomplish it.

They catch on quickly to the idea that if you are a kid who is
higher ranking than another kid it is your job to help the little ones,
not to boss them, and to watch out for them if they need it. So the
little ones feel safe and trust the bigger ones, and the bigger ones like
the responsibility and the status. They know they have earned their
status by their own hard work and they like the trust that the others
have in them.

They prove to each other and to themselves that they are strong. They become stronger. They respect each other, share challenges, become friends.

No one is acting out or giving anyone a hard time. Everyone is moving and learning and feeling alive. They are laughing sometimes, serious sometimes. The atmosphere changes through the class period from playful to focused effort, and back and forth. Sometimes the children move slowly and softly. They yell and they run. Sometimes they are silent and still.

Every culture finds its own ways to initiate children into adulthood. There are many different ways in which it is done but it will always demand self-mastery, disciplined skill training, and a testing which will require a letting go of the dependence and safety of childhood, and a taking up of the responsibility and freedom of adulthood. The experience can be painful. The method must be skillful. If the culture doesn't have a method of initiation into adulthood that works, then kids will make one up.

Lacking skill or experience, this impulse often goes wrong: hazing by fraternities or teams—forced drinking and drugging, torture, humiliation, violent gang rituals, and so on.

My friends and I tried to test our limits. As kids we ran around on roofs, jumped from overpasses, ran back and forth across eight lanes of high-speed traffic on the Expressway. We floated out into the bay on a piece of an old plank, and scaled the stone wall around the old Civil War fort that the Army had marked "Off Limits."

Watching out for rats, we climbed the chain link fence and slipped under the barbed wire, drenched in bay water, so we could run around in there and look for arrowheads and musket balls. We tried to drink. We fought. Later on we played football. We aspired to ace our classes.

Societies and individuals that handle initiation skillfully have mature adults as members. Those that don't, don't.

Some Native Americans took their teenage boys to a place far out in the wilderness and left them there. Sometimes they buried them up to the neck. Sometimes they were tied with strips of leather. Sometimes they were left on a rocky outcrop under the broiling sun and the immense night sky, without food or water, with only the company of wild animals and the unknown, alone for the first time, for days.

Outward Bound puts teenagers through high ropes courses. Mothers give birth. Medical students stay awake making life and death decisions for days at a time. Monks meditate all day every day for a week and almost never move. And they all know they can quit anytime. But they don't. The Navy SEALs stay awake and afloat in the crashing surf, training round the clock, carrying telephone pole sized logs or heavy rubber boats as they run, freezing, starving, exhausted and half drowned, while accessible to them at all times is a large brass bell. They can pull the rope on the bell at anytime and get out of the water and into the warmth and have a hot meal and a rest. And lose their chance to be a SEAL for good. They ring out or they don't. Some units put prospective team members through a test period during which they are deprived of sleep, food and water, travel huge distances through the ocean or the wild, come under fire, drop out of airplanes miles above the earth, open their parachutes seconds above the ground, rappel from helicopters into the ocean, remain under water till their lungs nearly burst, swim to shore, and then push the truck that brought them there back to the base.

Someone willing to go through these things, someone able to accomplish them, is a strong and dependable person. Go through it with them and you know you can count on them.

Mount Everest, a thousand mountain trails, canyons, caves, glaciers, deserts, rivers, oceans, sheer cliffs, and the urban underground are scoured by adventurers who walk them, climb them, sail them, haunt them, and challenge them. And not, "Because it's there," but because *they* are, and they want the pressure to grow on.

Doing what it takes to earn a degree, to compete in sports, to have a family, to succeed in business can be initiations into adulthood.

For young people to mature they need to try hard to enter a society of strong, older people. To enter they must be asked to prove themselves worthy. Strong in mind and body. And in character, too. Courage, determination, skills, dignity without arrogance are all traits that will help the young person gain admittance into the group. He will be needed. He will be someone with traits the group will rely on, if membership is conferred. Nobody wants to hang out with an emotionally dependent loser or a weenie. It's boring and, under pressure, it's dangerous.

There's a place for everyone in the world. No one should be harmed. But to have a good life and a good society people need to be encouraged to be strong and of good character. If they are not, everyone suffers.

Initiation is necessary. It happens in our karate dojo. Nothing is said about it. But parents see their sons and daughters go through it. And the comparison of a well-initiated teenager to a non-initiated one is convincing evidence that it works.

It may happen slowly, over years. Some signposts, like a black belt test, are part of it. In most cases it seems like initiation finds you when you are ready.

41. The Nature of a Cup

Here is an example: The smell of beer and cigarette smoke engulfed her as she tended the bar. She toweled down the splashes and the sticky circles on the old oak bar for the thousandth time that night. "So what are you doing after work tonight?," another dickhead inquired. To her the guys that sat at the bar were, "Men." To her they were not a particular subgroup of men, lonely alcoholics who occupied barstools and drank their lives away, guys who were unable to figure out that the women who worked at the bar were working, who could not grasp that their motivation was mainly money. These guys thought these women working there were hanging out with them.

She had to put up with them, she believed. Her habit was to think that life was something that happened to her, not something she went out and did. She worked as a bartender, floated along. It was boring. The patrons would say the same stupid things night after night. Sometimes she would refuse to serve them because they'd had enough, and they would get angry or threatening. She would get embarrassed, then frustrated as they persisted, then scared as their pickled tempers flared and threats flew.

She was tormented. Everything was personal. She felt like she was wrong. Unpleasant as it was, boring as it was, futureless as it was, she accepted it. She just kept working.

When the chance came to study abroad for her junior year in college, she grabbed it. She hoped there was something great out there. Days after arriving in a small town in Spain she met one of the other American students, a member of our dojo, who had been training with us for about four years at that time. Just before he left for his year of study abroad he had received his black belt.

At the time that he first joined the dojo he had been just hanging out. It was after his High School graduation, and he had nothing to show for it but an attitude and a job counting bugs in the basement of the science store. By this time, four years later, he had gone back to college, pleased to be on his own, away from home. He continued his karate practice during his junior year in Spain, every day.

She had never met anyone dedicated like that. He was totally into it. He told her she was welcome to join in.

Oh sure, she thought.

She could learn it.

Really?

He would teach her.

Okay....

He would be at the plaza nearby. It was up a long flight of steps. He said he would be there every morning at six. One morning she went. He was there. He showed her a few karate techniques. She practiced them. He said if you want to do this you do not do it casually. You do not miss training days. For any reason.

He encouraged her, every day. No demands, just encouragement. After each class, surprising herself, she thanked him, sincerely.

She had a feeling she never had before: today this man has really done something for me. Only a few weeks before, she had been a very nervous person. She was even nervous about the possibility of being nervous. And she tended to worry about that, too. She used to worry before she went out that the Spanish sun might get to her. But now, here she was out in it, every day.

One day some of her friends, American students studying in Europe for a semester, came to visit. Observing the local custom they started partying around midnight. They drank a lot and made it home as the sun was coming up. The friends crashed, but she took a shower, and as she was walking out of the apartment one of the friends mumbled, half asleep, "Where are you going?" and she said "I have to go to karate," and tiptoed quickly down the hall.

She carried a cup with her as she trudged up the hundreds of steep steps to the plaza for morning karate training, because she was so hung over she knew she was going to puke and she wanted the cup to catch it in. Civilized. Dedicated. Why? He made it fun. He made it feel important. He was dedicated. It was just a short time since she began to practice but her body had already changed. She was getting stronger. She felt alive.

She never worked in a bar again.

42. Bodhisattvas in the Diamond Net

One of the delights of Shakespeare or Tolstoy is that at the outset of their dramas they launch a multiplicity of intentions that operate in concert to form each dramatic moment, and play out coherently from many points of view. Good stories do not rely on the weak dramatic convention of a single character's intention that acts like a cue ball, initiating action in a world populated by people who are without independent motives, who exist only to respond to the actions of the main character. That kind of story tends to fail to engage or satisfy the audience. Beginner storytellers often start with this kind of one-dimensional tale.

We tend to start our lives like this too. We are born. We live in a world made exclusively of our own sensations. We are the focus of the attention of our family. We are protected by our family and by the stable shape of our community. We become self-centered. We act as if we are the center of the world, the main character in every story we are in. According to tradition, when the baby Buddha was born he looked forward and back, side to side. Then he took seven steps, lotuses sprouting up each time he lifted his foot. He said: "In all the universe I alone am the world-honored one!" Children are like this.

But after infancy this way of acting fails: it doesn't match the way other people see the world. We get frustrated. We feel isolated, we feel pain and we think it's the world's fault. Teenagers experience this. We yearn for happy relations with others. We change our view and our behavior. We become adults. But even as things in our lives work out better, as we feel more satisfied, we become aware of our impermanence. As we get old we sense that our lives are fading out, that we are destined to die. This feeling is at the heart of the religious impulse. Every culture has a way of addressing this spiritual need. As we come to grips with this reality we mature. We see the world through the eyes of others as well as through our own.

What it takes to tell a story with multiple perspectives, and what it takes to live a life engaged with other people, are both intelligence and heart. Feelings alone will not achieve results. And acute powers of perception alone, instead of leading to a great life, may lead to a manipulative one.

Intelligence and heart are seed forms of wisdom and compassion. In the Buddhist sense the implications of these terms are profound. Wisdom is the apprehension of the true nature of reality, complete and unobstructed in all space and all time. Compassion, ultimately, is a feeling of connection with other beings so deep it is as if every being is your only child, and you would do or give anything to help them.

Our ordinary human intelligence is a kind of wisdom. Caring about how someone is doing is a kind of compassion.

Beginning

Indecision

Searching

Training

Temptation

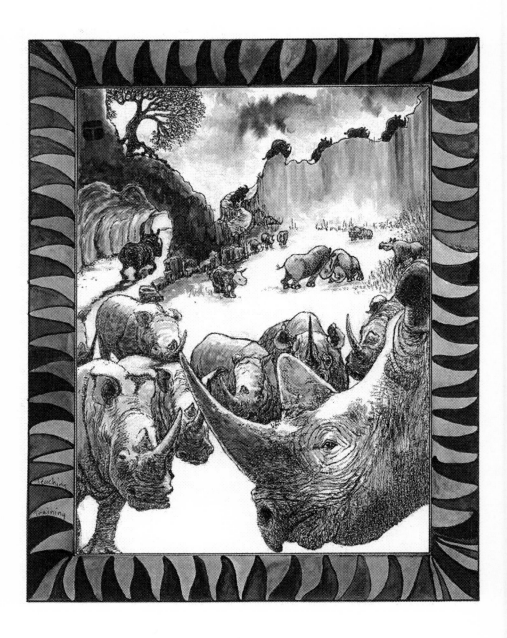

Teaching

Mastery

The fact that these feelings in us may be limited or tainted with self-interest does not invalidate them. We have these faculties. We can use them. We can cultivate them or let them decay.

Whether a person walks in to our dojo just because it is the nearest place to their house, or because they heard about it from a dozen people and have traveled past a dozen other dojos to get here, either way, we have an opportunity.

To teach you have to see that each person is walking in with a unique human life, with miraculous potential and with suffering. Sometimes I do not want to experience anyone else's fear, anger, need, inadequacy, power trips, manipulation, ambition, knee pain, flattery, timidity, frustration, vacillation, distraction, complacency, triumph, attachment to schedule, flippant attitude, cold, flu, hangnail, hangover or whatever it is. But these are all included in people's bodies and minds. That is the material we work with.

One day Takayoshi Nagamine, the son of the founder of our style, showed me a poem called the Kempo Haku, the Eight Verses on Karate. Eight lines of advice written in Chinese and included in the old collection of Okinawan martial arts literature called the Bubishi. In it is a line that advises karate practitioners, "You must hear the sounds from all four directions. You must see in all eight directions." These lines can be interpreted as listen carefully and be sure to watch your back. But there is more to it. We need to hear and see not only from our own subjective point of view. We need to lose that subjectivity and if we are actually to discern the seeds of coming events before they are manifest, if we will be effective in opposition or in aid, we need to encompass the potentiality in the moment, not just be caught in our own perceptions, habits, expectations and view.

How good I am at teaching depends on my willingness not just to be out there training, showing the students the form to follow, but to be sincerely engaged in my own practice, and to see practice from the perspective of the people I am practicing with. I need to have the heart to care, and the wisdom to act skillfully on their behalf.

In scripture there are lots of stories about the acts of Buddhas-in-training who endure great hardships for the sake of others. As a practitioner it is a fact of life that we continually have to choose what we value more: enlightenment or comfort.

To train well you have to use your body, skillfully. You have to take good care of it. If you are conditioning your legs to become powerful, or if you are sitting long hours in meditation, you will get sore. You have to decide what is more important, comfort or the rewards of training?

A few months after I started karate I quit smoking. I was 21. I did not want to quit. But I had to make the choice: be able to do karate and all the other things I liked to do or smoke. I did not want to sacrifice practice for smoking. So to meet the demands of practice I changed.

One kid who was pretty fat when he joined our dojo decided he really liked karate and wanted to be good at it. He came to class every day (his choice) and his Mom told me there was a moment when he made his choice: One day he sat down with a bag of

Doritos and flipped on a movie about basketball. It seemed to
dawn on him, she said, that he was not doing what the guys in the
movie were doing. He was eating and watching, they were training,
playing and having adventures. He put the Doritos away... and did
some pushups.

He thought of himself as being in training, and that changed his
actions. It changed his karate too and, step by step, his life got better.
The story he told himself about himself changed to the story of a
kid in training, a kid with possibilities, a kid who could triumph over
ordinariness.

According to tradition a former general in the Chinese Imperial
Army, seeking instruction, waited for along time in the snow outside
the cave where the great Indian Buddhist master Bodhidharma, was
meditating. The General was a powerful man. He devoted his life
to protecting his country, but now he appealed to Bodhidharma for
instruction in meditation, the only thing, the General knew, that
could provide ultimate protection.

Bodhidharma refused. Even sitting still in the snow for days
was not enough of a demonstration of sincerity and determination.
The General cut off his arm and offered it to Bodhidharma.
Bodhidharma accepted him as his student. That's how the story
goes. Is this an act of barbaric self-mutilation? Is it like the mafia
cutting off the fingertip of the inductee? Is it the slavish self-
effacement of someone desperate for someone else to lead him
through life? No. To attain profound insight into our nature we have
to overcome attachment to what we conventionally assume is me:
my body, my comfort, my status and so on.

Zen Master Dogen brought the Silent Illumination or Soto school of Zen from China to Japan in the 13th century. He described enlightenment as simply "dropping off body and mind." In the Pali sutras—the early collection of the Buddha's talks written in the Pali language—the Buddha teaches that one way to break the chain of dependent origination and so bring an end to suffering, is by cutting the link of "body and mind." What does that mean? Suicide? Certainly not. The opposite in fact.

There is one ancient story that tells about a man who has no money to offer to a teacher in exchange for teaching. He is so intent upon studying that he cuts the flesh off his own arms and tries to sell it in the market place. He calls out to the passersby in the marketplace but a demon has made his voice inaudible. Tears pour down his face. Not from the pain of cutting off his flesh, but because, according to the story, he is frustrated that no one can hear

him. Without money to offer he can't approach a teacher properly
and so learn to practice dharma—the teachings of the Buddha
on morality, meditation and wisdom that constitute the path to
enlightenment. Eventually his voice is heard and he fulfills his wish.
Is the story too repellant to be inspiring to modern people? Is
this merely and ancient allegory intended to turn gullible would-
be devotees into slaves of the clergy? Put the question this way:
what causes us to suffer? What does it take for suffering to cease?
Allegorically and in fact, the limited pain of the body we may
experience in this life is nothing compared to the suffering of the
"samsaric cycle": birth, suffering, sickness, old age and death,
repeated endlessly. Suffering will come to an end when we let go
of our mistaken understanding of the way in which we exist. And
only then.

And why do these stories keep talking about arms?

A woman in our dojo was training for several years. She was
consistent in her practice, getting through the occasional bout of
sore muscles, quaking knees and bruised forearms that are standard
for beginners. She became healthy. She felt strong. The dojo had
become her place. Then one day she was paired off for partner
practice with a fellow who heads another dojo. He is a generous
teacher whose imagination and hard work has year after year
inspired many long-time practitioners.

Faced off for partner practice he performed a technique in a
way this woman had never experienced before. He went too far for
her. It made her elbow swollen and sore. It stayed that way week
after week. She couldn't even throw a punch. She couldn't bend it

much or straighten it out. She couldn't practice. She cursed him in her mind again and again. Soon I noticed that she was modifying certain moves in her kata and I said, "Hey, what's going on?" She was mad at me too. How could I let this happen? How could karate do this to her? She was just a nice person, doing things right, and the person who hurt her was a man, a big one, a more advanced one! How could I permit this!?

It wasn't her doing, she felt. I knew she didn't sit in the snow and cut her own arm off to make a statement. But she put herself in the position she was in in order to learn karate. Her intention, in training, was to change. Up until this moment the challenges to her body and mind had come in carefully calibrated increments and now here was a pressure that was not so carefully applied. It caused her pain. Here's all I could say: "I am sorry he hurt you. Do not expect the people you are faced off with to always be careful with you. They will make mistakes. They will misjudge. Sometimes they will go too hard. Sometimes they will be too soft, and you will be lulled into complacency. Be ready. Be aware of how little it takes to hurt someone. If you are ever attacked it will be valuable information. For you to carry around this rage with you for week after week does not hurt him. It hurts you. So heal up, don't pass on the mistake to others, and keep your training strong."

One time a kid in the juvenile offender program remained outside the dojo door after the rest of his group had come inside. He was new. I went out and asked him, hey, aren't you taking karate today? He said no, I want to, but my arm hurts. He held it up. There were bandages around part of his hand but I could see several hack marks on his forearm and wrist, scarred but healing. There were some purplish hack marks across his fingers, healed in a bent and distorted way. I could see where they had been stitched. He said "I got cut with a machete. So I have to let it heal."

This kid didn't "get cut." He had his hand in front of him for protection and it looked like he was hacked ten times, maybe twenty. I asked him, so do you think you will stay out of trouble for a while? He said, yeah, about one month more. One month? I assumed he would not want to repeat this. He said yeah, but… his mind wandering, he continued, you know if I had a martial arts school I would take two guys and lock them in the room and they would have to fight to the death. And the one that got killed I would spit on him. And the one that lived would be my hero. He looked at me and he seemed to expect me to say that's great, you really understand what martial arts is all about. But I said look, anyone can harm or smash anyone else. That doesn't take any brains or training or courage. In martial arts you learn to protect yourself, and protect other people. You get the power to do the right thing. That's what martial arts is all about.

He seemed to be listening carefully. As if he had never heard this kind of thing before.

That kid used his arms to protect himself. He willingly, without reflecting, jeopardized them to save his life. We use our arms to protect, to grasp, push away, cling to, hold on, manipulate, and so on. Our arms mediate between our sense of "me" in here and the world, out there. Metaphorically and in fact we use our reach and our grasp to obtain and manipulate what we think of as being "out there" and in this effort we reinforce a mental habit of moving away from here and now, continually trying to adjust our universe, mistaking the nature of the objects we try to manipulate, and so distance ourselves from our real lives.

43. Arms and the Man

I like to meditate because it makes it easy to see that the events of my life are not the extent of my life. I can see my karma in action. I can see that the things I do and the circumstances in which I find myself, in the way I respond and in the way things shift, are the result of my action. In sitting meditation I am free to go beyond subjective experience. Sitting provides a context in which to live.

One day I got sued. The demand letter had appeared three times over three years but now the suit was filed. A fellow got a broken arm one day, practicing at my dojo with one of the instructors. I was not there when it happened. But when I came back from lunch I saw the two of them dressed and leaving the dojo. I usually return from my lunch break around one o'clock. The class is scheduled to go to 1:15. They were talking nicely. The instructor seemed unusually placid and so did the student. During partner practice they heard the student's arm make a popping sound, and then the student's arm hurt. So now, as I walked in, the instructor was taking this man to the hospital to get it checked out.

The suit accuses the instructor of assault and battery, with malice, and wanton disregard. They accused me of breach of contract and fraud. The breach of contract seemed to be that I did not tell the fellow he could get a broken arm, the fraud was that in our yellow pages ad we offer peace of mind. He didn't get it.

So it is us against them after all! He didn't want his arm to end up broken. I didn't want to get my livelihood taken away. Lawsuits in professional life are like boredom in practice life, facts of life we prefer not to discuss. But they are the eight hundred pound gorillas in the room. They influence on us, acknowledged or not.

The prospect of losing everything is not good. But eventually we are all going to lose everything. We are all going to lose our homes and our bank accounts and our status and our livelihood, our jobs and our families, our bodies and good looks and thoughts and senses and everything else we care about and depend upon and think of as ours, as ourselves—and we will lose these things without the chance to go back and learn a new trade and get a new start.

Unless our practice goes deep enough to free us forever from suffering, the end will come. And we tend to ignore that inevitability. It does not produce a feeling of dread or urgency. We treat it as if it were external to our lives, a given, meaningless because unstoppable and universal. Relative misfortune causes us great concern—the loss of power, loss of status, embarrassment. Absolute misfortune is off our radar.

But it is of utmost concern, right now, for all of us. We would be best off to live our lives in light of it, not in spite of it. And so the lawsuit is good. Come on. Painful to me as a broken arm is to him? What about the feeling of our hands grasping on to dear life when dear life is yanked away? If we cling too tightly to the conditional aspects of our lives we lose our chance at freedom; we give our lives up to a mirage. If we have a context in which we can clearly see the events of our lives, in which we can see our karma in operation, in which we can see the indispensable value of virtuous action, then we will not throw our lives away. That is why deep practice is indispensable.

44. The Monk with the Woman in his Arms

For a few months when my divorce was pending I lived on
a platform, among the boxes of karate uniforms and other dojo
supplies I keep on hand, above my office. I wouldn't admit I would
never return "home." I imagined what it would be like if the sun
were to set on life. Eyesight dimming. Breath getting shallow. One
by one the thoughts come across your mind of each one of the
things you have done and people you have loved. You see all the
faces of each person you knew and now will never see again. Now
at this moment of farewell each one of them looks more and more
like a miraculous thing, a wonder. How could you have missed all
this before? Then, each of their faces fading out. Each sensation
your last sensation: of that air, the sunlight, the trees you watched,
the clouds blowing by, the touch of a hand, a hand of someone
you love. It comes as a surprise. Can it be over? I have never had
the experience of my life being over before. I have had a day end.
A weekend. A love. But not the whole thing. No more chances
to get it right. No more of any of it. No more strength. No more
disappointments, no more delights. No more rest. All the worries,
over. Who will protect the people I care for? The cold seeps in. Did
I do it right? Was it all right? Darkening. Don't want to go. I was
happy here. Can't use my body any more. I am very used to it. Even
when it hurt. That was my body. My legs. My arms. My hands. My
feet. I am used to them. I always had them. Now I can't have it any
more. What to make of it? Who to tell? On my own again, after all
this time. I hear the river. I feel my heartbeat.

A little while before a group of Tibetan monks had come to our
town and made a sand mandala at the edge of a pond formed where

the river that runs across from the dojo is dammed and rises a few feet. People came to watch the monks at work on the edge of the pond. Day after day, when people came to that spot, they saw the monks, with deep concentration, working. Day after day they saw the mandala taking shape and growing in size, in complexity, in detail, in beauty. People wonder (even if they never ask the graceful dignified monks making the sand mandalas) after all the weeks of meticulous work to create the beautiful map of the universe in a dozen colors, grain of sand by grain of sand why then, at the end of the ceremonial period, do you just blow it all away, blow it away with hand held fans till the grains of sand fly off into the pond and the colors mingle on the ground, in the air in the water, as the mandala fades and dissolves and very soon disappears. Why not save it? And the monks might say, "This is how life goes. This mandala depicts what is happening to you, little by little, right now. It is going to happen completely, at the end of your life. The life we live thinking it will last forever, the life we are painstakingly year after year, moment after moment, carefully creating in meticulous detail, with all our comforts and yearning, clothing and car payments, the house cleaning, the tooth brushing, status seeking, education, family, career—all the little grains of life we carefully assemble as if they would always stay in place, as if they were the most important thing, as if they would never blow away, fade, disappear."

I stood in the moonlight watching the river. It was midnight and still warm. I heard a car engine coming from around the side of the building where there should have been no sound. Someone showing up at midnight. Driving right up. We said good night hours ago. That was it. We decided. Here she was. I was happy. I had not factored this happiness in when I planned my future. In two days I was leaving for Okinawa.

When she, my beloved, dropped me off at the airport I was as cool as could be. I had just come back from the edge of extinction, no money, no home, no family, living on a shelf in the dojo, imagining life ebbing out of my cells, when I was resurrected in the glory of one true love. Happy ending! But now I was leaving.

The plane took off, but the bungee cords of love held fast. They stretched across the plains, over the coast, and across the ocean. I found an empty section in the back of the 747. When the lights were dimmed and everyone on the plane was asleep I went back there and did kata in the aisle, in slow motion, unnoticed, alone.

When you are young your training will be focused on personal perfection but as you mature that changes. You don't abandon that. You build on it.

This was one of the stories in the little Zen book on my sixth grade teacher's desk. Here's how I remember it: Two monks were walking down the road in China, a thousand years ago. The roads were not paved and people traveled by foot or by cart. As they do today in some parts of Asia, the monks lived a peripatetic life, traveling from temple to temple. They set out on the roads just after the rainy season, when their three-month period of secluded meditation practice was over.

There were puddles on the roads. At the edge of one puddle stood a beautiful young woman, dressed in silk. She was waiting at the edge of the puddle because she did not want to ruin her clothes. She hoped maybe an ox cart would come by soon and she could get a ride across. The two monks saw her standing there.

To understand the significance of this moment here's a little backstory: Buddhist monks were celibate. Since these were Chinese monks they would have taken the monks' vows as well as a second set of vows called the bodhisattva vows. The monks' vows are called "pratimoksha" vows in Sanskrit. Prati means individual, moksha translates as freedom. These are strict rules designed to give the monks complete freedom from the attachments and disturbances of ordinary life that would prevent them from meditating deeply. In India, for example, monks were obligated by their vows to beg for their food. They were not permitted to eat after noon. They were not permitted to work. Or even to farm. Sometimes they would be given gifts of money or cloth. The rules prohibited monks from keeping the cloth unless they needed it to make a robe. In India, in the early centuries of Buddhism, it was warm. The monks' vows limited the amount of clothes a monk could have to three robes.

These rules may sound restrictive, but monks who follow them today say that the rules are a source of freedom. They are free to live simply, to meditate, to be still. The rules were changed slightly in China in later centuries because, for example, monasteries were sometimes located in remote areas, so they had to support themselves with farming or gardening. And it was cold up there in the mountains, so it was not practical for them to have only three thin robes to wear.

The pratimoksha vows prohibited sexual contact, or even the appearance of the possibility of it. Monks were not to go into people's homes. They were not to meet alone with women. In fact there is a rule that prohibits even sleeping under the same roof as a woman. The nuns' vows treat their contact with men in the same way. This was designed to free them from disturbance, although it is hard for modern people to imagine it would work that way. We might imagine that they were constantly disturbed by sexual desire. Some of them, especially the younger ones, were. In modern times the very idea of celibacy has become suspect; more likely to be associated with scandal and hypocrisy than genuine spiritual aspiration or peace. It has been badly taught and misused. The practice of celibacy is not something that can be governed simply by the will.

In those days those monks ate very little, and never after noon. They slept little and stayed up late in meditation, so they were often hungry and tired. Their metabolisms cooled down. In those conditions sexual desire subsides. Those monks lived in a communal setting in which they were surrounded by fellow practitioners who respected this way of life. Their focus was on practice, the results they could achieve and the austerity that supported it. They understood the use of celibacy, and valued it. This ideal was not met in every case. But it did inform the culture and the practice of those monks.

The goal of people who held pratimoksha vows was to purify their minds and achieve the permanent cessation of all mental disturbance. That is nirvana. In some later Buddhist traditions, including Ch'an, the Chinese precursor of Japanese Zen, this is considered to be a provisional, incomplete goal. It does not represent the highest perfection of human life. That ultimate goal is Buddhahood: the permanent cessation of mental disturbance in a mind permeated with the desire to save all beings.

In some of these later traditions (and down to the present day in the Mahayana traditions of China and Tibet, for example) monks also take a second set of vows. These are called the bodhisattva vows. Instead of focusing only on the task of liberating themselves from suffering, a "bodhisattva" vows to save all beings from suffering. In part the bodhisattva vows are also concerned with personal restraint. In fact they include the kinds of prohibitions found in the pratimoksha vows. Not killing, not stealing, not lying, not engaging in sexual misconduct, not using intoxicants, not gossiping, not criticizing, not being greedy, not being angry, not holding on to false views. Unlike the pratimoksha vows the bodhisattva vows do not require practitioners to separate themselves entirely from the world, but rather to act in it.

Practicing in this way, the putative conflict between what benefits me and what benefits others is revealed to be fiction.

The two Chinese Mahayana monks walking down the muddy road had taken both sets of vows. Sometimes a choice must be made. The demands of one vow must supersede the demands of another.

Back to the story: The two monks see the beautiful sexy young woman standing by the muddy puddle. One monk keeps his eyes down and begins to cross the mud. The other monk speaks to the lady: "Need a lift?" She nods. He scoops her up in his arms and carries her over the water. At the other side of the puddle he sets her down. The monk says: "Have a nice day" and off they go down the road.

Later that evening, after many hours walking in silence, the monk who had carried the lady says to the other monk: "Let's go stay in that shelter over there for the night." The other monk however was so angry he could hardly speak. He stops in his tracks, turns on his companion and almost shouts "How could you do that?! How could you touch that woman! You have broken your vows, you are defiled, you have ruined your chance at enlightenment and you are going to be thrown out of the community of monks!"

According to the pratimoksha vows that interpretation would have been correct. But the carrying monk said "I put her down hours ago. You've been carrying her around all day."

Is this old story a story about desire? About common sense? About kindness? About attachment? In karate practice we approach these issues not with explanation but with direct experience. If, in a sparring match you throw a punch that misses, and you linger even for a split second on the error, you will get hit. If you land a technique and get distracted by its effect on your opponent you will immediately lose the advantage you gained by it, and also run the risk of getting hit. As you practice you develop a habit of neither projecting out into the future—planning your next move or looking for an opportunity—or lingering in the past. You are able to forget about the past and future and engage in the fresh dynamic of the present.

It is useful to examine our action. See what worked or what didn't. We need to plan, too. We should consider what results our actions may have in the future. That is essential. However, it is possible to consider the past or the future as the work of this moment, instead of getting lost in drifting imagination.

The story of the two monks and the beautiful woman is partly about attachment. The Carrying Monk instructs the Angry Monk on the subject. It is easy to see this point about attachment because it is this conflict that is revealed and resolved at the end of the story. The Angry Monk was attached to his own purity and his own vow. The story shows it to be a narrow view, which causes him increased disturbance—the opposite of what he hoped for.

The Carrying Monk's story is more interesting. That is a story about vow and bodhisattva action. The Carrying Monk's action did not derive its meaning from the observer's judgment of it. He would appear to any observer, in that place and time, like a monk misbehaving. But his motivation may well have been to help the

lady, not to hug her for the pleasure of it. He may have had a
nice time holding her. And if he did, according to the story, he
experienced the pleasurable sensation and then later the pleasurable
sensation ceased. As a sincere practitioner he may have legitimately
been concerned that he was jeopardizing his equanimity by having
this pleasurable experience. He might be risking the benefit that
could come from years of sitting in meditation with this one
moment of pleasurable experience, because from now on he might
waste his practice time fantasizing about her.

But it may well be that he did not think of himself first. Perhaps
he thought: Here is an opportunity to help this person. If his
motivation was to hug the woman, he broke a pratimoksha vow. If
his motivation was to help her he upheld a bodhisattva vow. Only
he would be sure. He was sure. His action was mature. He was not
looking for outside approval. No credit would come to him. He was
practicing as a bodhisattva, and the act itself was spontaneously
right. Understood this way we can see that it had good results for his
practice, for the woman on her journey, and he added to the angry
monk's understanding, too.

As for the woman's story? Maybe she was careless. Maybe
she was flirting with them. Maybe she was stranded and in urgent
need of help so she could get on her way. Maybe she was a demon
tempting them. Maybe she was a Buddha, skillfully helping these
two monks, in two completely different ways.

Monk or not, the story is useful for all of us. Who hasn't held
on to a thought—a grudge, a regret, a hope, desire—and allowed
it to disturb us, long after we could have let it go? You can practice

letting disturbing thoughts go. You can get good at it. Sitting in meditation is a way to do it. You can do it by cultivating samadhi, deep concentration, in karate practice as well.

Kindness and self-restraint helps to free us from the suffering caused by our own ignorance, meanness and greed. It is a serious business. It demands a high degree of awareness and self-control. And not just for an hour a day in meditation, but all the time. Studying the vows will tell you what actions bring suffering and what actions end suffering. Meditation practice lets you monitor the condition of your mind, so you can be aware of what you are doing. This kind of healthy self-discipline is the source of human freedom.

There is a line that comes in the midst of a traditional chant used in Zen practice centers in both Asia and the west. It comes in the midst of what is essentially a list of meditation instructions. It says "Do not distinguish between good and evil." This line has been taken out of context and misunderstood by people both inside and outside the world of Zen. Critics use it to prove that Zen has no morality. This is a false interpretation. However, credence is given to their argument by the behavior of ignorant Zen practitioners. They misinterpret this line to justify acting on any impulse that seems pleasing to them at the moment.

The line comes in a list of advice on how to practice zazen. Cross your legs. Fold your hands. Sit tall, mouth closed, and so on. You can be still and at peace. If you are sitting in proper posture your mind will naturally settle down. You don't even have to try. In fact trying to stop the activity of your mind by conscious effort is like trying to stamp out the waves on the surface of a pool by smashing them down with your hand. It makes it worse.

So in that daily chant we are presented with this instruction to "make no distinction between good and evil." It was devised especially for monks who have been training under pratimoksha, and who are moving on to bodhisattva level. It is addressed to practitioners who may have been operating under the unquestioned assumption that their effort ought to be aimed directly and exclusively at the purification of disturbance from their own mind. The instruction tells them that for now, while seated in meditation, when you cannot speak, when you cannot move, when the gates of karma are sealed shut, don't even get involved with the thoughts your mind is producing. Don't attach to them, judge them, consider them as being of any importance. The thoughts will arise. Let them subside. Be peaceful.

That is the point of "make no distinction between good and evil." That is a meditation instruction. We could talk about the same statement from a metaphysical point of view, observing that no phenomena have objective reality that is not contingent upon the karma of the observer. Here we have an example of an inclusive principle (emptiness of all phenomena) negating absolute opposition (good and evil.) That is like saying God sees everything, or the universe includes everything. Those propositions negate absolute opposition too.

But this does not imply there is no difference between the opposites. There is a universe of difference between them. If you are cruel you suffer and others suffer. If you are kind you ease the suffering of others and your own suffering subsides as well. To act on this basis is imperative. It is the meaning of the bodhisattva vow. Good and evil are not the same at all. They are both within the reality of our experience, within our lives. Like love. Like separation.

45. Okinawa in the Ocean of Time

There are ascetic practices in which your metabolism is turned way down and you can barely tell what is holding you to life. You experience sensations in an unusual way—with the usual boundary between yourself and what you see, what you hear, and what you think almost gone. It feels almost as if light passes through you, as if sounds blow through you without resistance, almost without contact. You feel like you are nothing other than a stream of perceptions. This can happen in intensive training in karate. Also after meditating for a while without eating much, without sleeping much, without moving much. Intensive training in a monastery schedule can produce this. It is not a goal of spiritual practice in itself, but it permits a direct observation of the way our mind operates that is otherwise unattainable and which is a necessary prerequisite for understanding how our mind influences the way we experience reality.

The last time I saw Sakiyama Roshi was the morning I left Okinawa. I went to Kozenji early for 6 a.m. zazen. The streets were damp and had the used look old cities get when the light first comes up. You can see, without people on the sidewalk and traffic obscuring the pavement, all the things you'd never notice at the height of a busy day. At dawn the city appears as a backdrop, unplanned but perfectly prepared, for the performance of daily life.

The signs on storefronts, written in Japanese, announced low prices and big sales.

Naha, the capital of Okinawa, was still. The sun appeared above the sea.

Naha felt familiar. Karate was less visible on the streets of Okinawa than it is in the average American city. In Okinawa karate is, for the most part, still practiced privately, in homes, in small groups, which form by word of mouth, the old way, by the recommendation of a friend or through family connections. Not by answering an ad in the yellow pages, or seeing a sign on a storefront or a mall.

Shoshin Nagamine's dojo occupies a converted garage, attached to his home and family grocery store, on a quiet street in a residential neighborhood. A second floor room above an appliance store, where some of the most accomplished practitioners on the island gathered to train a few nights a week, was a bare room, with nothing more to mark it as a dojo than a few framed photos on the wall. Another dojo I trained in was the backyard of a businessman's house, a flat gravel area cleared out between the tropical trees. Another was the living room of a professor's house. No signs.

Some of the names of the men teaching in these places are familiar to karate practitioners around the world. When they hold seminars in the US, hundreds attend. At home they have a handful of students and a quiet life.

I walked up Naha's steep streets at dawn toward Shuri Castle and the Kozenji Zen Temple. The florescent lights in the vending machines selling cans of cold coffee at the bus stop were fading in the dawn as I reached the top of the hill.

There the city streets stop. Above me were the walls of the castle. More a cliff than a building, huge stone blocks stacked tight and tall, seamless, an imposing impression of permanence and power, a sign that here was the heart of the kingdom, and that it was unassailable.

I looked down. The ocean glinted in the dawn far off to the horizon in every direction. No boats yet. A spectacle beckoning, like it always had every morning, to generation after generation of the island's children growing up in the small safety of the kingdom, as they looked out on the ocean and imagined the world out there.

Mostly the world out there was China. How did they think of it? Wonderful? Vast? The real world? The source? A big, powerful, strange, foreign place of unlimited possibility? Each year a few dozen of the children of the island's elite went to China, becoming suddenly anonymous foreign students in the heart of the empire, there to prepare for a lifetime of leadership back home.

They had been groomed for this since birth. They began their education at five years old. Ten years later, if they passed the rigorous qualifying exams, they traveled to Beijing on scholarship.

It was at Kumemura, Okinawa's China Town, where they prepared for their exams. They studied language, art, philosophy, etiquette, everything they would need when they went to study at the Imperial City. They studied with Chinese teachers and their Okinawan disciples. China Town was central to Okinawan cultural life from the 14th century until the Japanese occupation in the 19th.

Scholars and military personnel were sent by the Chinese government to live on Okinawa. Chinese visitors spread the civilizing influence of the Middle Kingdom to the distant corners of the world; even to this little tropical island in the middle of the eastern sea. The Chinese also taught, and gathered information. They kept a lookout for the Japanese. They made use of Okinawa's strategic position for commercial and military purposes, just as the Japanese did after 1897, and as the Americans have since 1946.

They made good use of the Okinawans' unrivaled sailing and navigational skills. The Chinese taught the provincials the essentials of civilized life: architecture, agriculture, art, administration, language, religion, and philosophy. In the mix came martial arts. A staple of the military training of the day was hand-to-hand combat, along with battlefield strategy, the use of arms—sword, spear, halberd—and cavalry. The use of empty hand fighting technique became a primary interest of the military elite during the time of Okinawan King Sho Shin.

King Sho Shin, Shoshin Nagamine's namesake, was the first Buddhist king of Okinawa. The fifty years of his reign (1477– 1526) were the golden age of Okinawan history. Karate rose in importance during his reign in part because he banned the carry of weapons in public. For the first time on the islands he instituted the rule of law, with courts replacing local armed conflict and aristocratic decree as the means of settling disputes. This eliminated the constant warfare between landowners, and not incidentally, consolidated power at his court. Sho Shin also required all the feudal lords to move to the capital, leaving their employees to manage their land. These innovations predated by more than a century similar policies used by the Tokugawa Shoguns in Japan to centralize authority and reduce civil war.

The practice of empty hand skills spread. Taught through the king's guard to their soldiers; taught by Chinese visitors to the sailors at the port of Naha and to residents of Kumemura and by the Chinese in Kumemura to Okinawan students. Various forms of martial arts, many imported directly from or influenced by the styles of mainland China, were practiced by aristocrats, soldiers, farmers and sailors and often mixed with their own indigenous fighting traditions.

Every two years a tribute ship loaded with gifts for the Emperor, crafts and other goods for sale, sailed to China. The ship also carried a delegation of Okinawan aristocrats, and the students selected for training on the mainland.

Ships sailed frequently from Okinawa to Chinese ports, to the Philippines, all over south Asia, to Indonesia, Malaysia and India. The prosperity of the island depended on the goods these ships carried.

The reputation of traders, then as now, depends on their ability to deliver. The Okinawans were high rollers. Sea travel was risky but the payback was worth it: Okinawan traders could realize returns of 1,000% or more on the investments they made in goods purchased at one port and sold at another.

The island had few resources of its own. People could barely grow enough food for themselves. That was why, as trade opportunities expanded, the government encouraged people to become artisans, to manufacture luxury goods. The profits from the sale of these goods were used to import food. Okinawan hand-crafting is still practiced today: hand woven and dyed kasuri cloth, and lacquer ware. One craftsman assured me his work would last at least 500 years. He wasn't bragging. Many examples have.

The Okinawans' dependence on trade increased over time, and they bet heavily on every boat that left port. Okinawa was like Venice, Lisbon, London, or Amsterdam — cosmopolitan city-states whose wealth and power grew from thriving foreign trade. Because of their international connections and their rapid accumulation of wealth the Okinawans had the need for and access to the most powerful fighting skills in the world.

The Okinawan historical records housed at Shuri Castle were destroyed during World War II when the castle was bombed. However records from the Chinese court and from trading partners like Korea still exist. And there are comments on Ryukyu Island culture in the notebooks of Portuguese Jesuits, the first and only westerners on Okinawa for centuries.

Okinawa was one of 60 countries that traded at Malacca in the early 15th century. The Jesuits noted that it was the Okinawans who transported tea from China to the court of the Japanese Shoguns. They also brought books and ceramics from Korea. In Japan the Okinawans loaded their ships with swords, lacquer ware, fans, screens and herbs. In the southern islands they traded those goods for coins, rare woods, exotic spices and incense, rhinoceros horn, iron, tin, sugar, gold, copper, silk, damask, porcelain, musk, along with grain and vegetables.

According to the Portuguese their Asian trading partners regarded the Okinawans the way the Europeans regarded the Milanese: as suppliers of the finest luxury goods in the world.

According to Malaysian records the Okinawans were scrupulously honest and demanded honesty. They delivered accurately, according to the bills of lading, without fail. They were willing to deal on credit. They expected to be paid in full, on time. If they weren't, or if they felt they were being cheated, they would immediately return to collect what was due to them, heavily armed. They would not deal in slaves or women. And they would not sell their own people for any price. They would fight to the death without hesitation if this were demanded of them. The Portuguese noted that they were always dignified, well dressed and rich. And they were utterly ferocious in self-defense. So aggressive and so successful were the Okinawans in defeating pirate attacks on their vessels that ships from other countries from time to time were observed flying the Okinawan flag, in the hopes that the pirates, who were thick along the trading routes of the East China Sea, would stay away.

This is an even more remarkable measure of the Okinawan character because visitors to the island invariably noted that the Okinawans were the happiest, most peaceful people they had encountered, anywhere in the world.

The symbol on the Okinawan flag is the "mitsu-domoe"— turning to the right. Before the mid 15th century, when it was adopted as the Okinawan royal family crest, it was the symbol of Hachiman, the Japanese god of war. The pirates in the area revered Hachiman and flew this symbol on their ships. Some people say the king of Okinawa was defying the pirates, refusing to yield the power of Hachiman to them.

The Okinawan golden age did not last. By the 16th century the Okinawan trading empire was in decline. Islam had crushed the Hindu states to the south. Japan was in anarchy: civil war was raging, its great cities were in flame, fields were filled with bodies, and villages were filled with dread. Europeans arrived, seeking gold, spices and souls. When the Okinawan trading mission arrived in Malacca for their annual visit in 1511 they found the once-prosperous city burned to the ground, the Portuguese fleet anchored in the harbor.

Still, the Okinawans' relationship with China, as a protected client state, held till the end of the 19th century. For reasons of politics and island culture, training in karate and individual armed combat remained a necessity.

Various karate traditions were associated with the leading families in Okinawan society, and entering into the study of one of these traditions brought prestige by association with the family as well as through accomplishment in karate itself. Some evidence of the tradition remains now. The name of the royal family was "Sho" through most of Okinawan history. Members of the royal clan who were not immediate members of the family of the king and so could not use the royal surname added the syllable "Cho" to their personal name.

The character Cho is written almost the same as Sho. Many karate teachers born in the generations before WWII were named using this convention, an indication of their aristocratic descent. Shoshin Nagamine was born amid the remnants of that feudal milieu. Most of the early lineage holders in our style have the syllable Cho or Sho in their name.

Decades after the departure of the Chinese from Okinawa's Kumemura, after the annexation of Okinawa Prefecture by the Imperial Japanese government in 1879, the practice of karate became reinforced as a symbolic as well as a practical pursuit for the Okinawan people. The benefits of practice were known and sought out for their own sake. For many practitioners in these years it had a deep personal and cultural dimension as well.

Even while a simplified form of karate was being introduced in the Okinawan public schools, most training in real karate continued take place in secret, in gardens and teacher's homes, in pine groves or on beaches, in inlets hidden among the rocks and surf, at night, or in the networks of limestone caverns and tunnels that snake for miles under the island. Karate training was a statement of cultural identity and independence. With Japanese military personnel, foreigners, strutting through the streets, humiliating the people, stealing their possessions, carting off the wealth of the nation, wiping out Okinawan culture, even discouraging the Okinawans from speaking their own language, the secret practice of karate became an expression of defiance, of strength and dignity in the face of the occupation by a hostile and degrading military force.

People still use karate this way on Okinawa, and in other parts of the world.

Standing there at the top of the hill near Shuri Castle, near the driveway leading down to Kozenji Zendo, I was thinking about how this must have appeared to someone on this beautiful tropical island, years ago, when they looked out to sea. What promise. What would it have been like for them the day they set out to sea, after anticipating that moment for all your life, hearing the stories of the men who went and came back, seeing what they brought, forming an impression of that world, noting the difference between the tales of the aristocrats who visited Beijing, and the sailors returning from the port of Fuchow? Maybe heading out was a thrill. Or a terror. Depending on what? Your personality? Your purpose? The weather? Politics? What did all that ocean mean?

The tourists I saw on Okinawa sure loved it, lying on their blankets on the beach, oiled and bikinied. To mainland Japanese people nowadays the ocean at Okinawa means beach resorts and party time. But down at the southern tip of the island the ocean has a totally different meaning. The world there, near the village of Itoman, feels silent and still. All you hear is the wind whipping in from the Pacific, accelerating up the sheer rock cliffs, and streaming through the beach grass on the hill. There is the Peace Memorial. Acres of dark gray granite blocks arrayed in ranks and files. Etched into each stone are names of the people who died during the battle of Okinawa. Hundreds of thousands of names. The American names are there. The Japanese names. The memorial is only a few hundred yards from the spot where the Japanese generals Ushijima and Cho, commanding the forces on Okinawa, in defeat, committed hara-kiri. Each cut into the bare flesh of his lower abdomen. Then with ceremonious precision their designated seconds cut off their heads, each with a single stroke of a sword.

The names of a hundred thousand Okinawan dead are recorded there in stone. A third of the population. Almost all civilians. Among them are the names of most of the masters of the old, secret karate.

The ocean looks different at Itoman. There is no expectation here in its vastness. Peace? Just a vastness that takes in everything, swallows everything, dissolves everything, includes everything. Whatever horror happened here has sunk, deep, deep, and disappeared. The ocean took it. The waves closed over it. The ocean is the same.

46. Sakiyama's Silence

As I left Kozenji temple Sakiyama Roshi saw me off. That day, in his flowing Zen robes, he walked with me a way down the street. We could see the ocean filled with ships now, far below. We walked a block, two blocks. I felt he wanted to say something to me. Because we did not share a language maybe he could not express what he wanted to say. Or because at such a time it is impossible to capture the sense in words, even in your own language. I was silent too. Anything I could have said would have been extra. I thanked him. He wished me well. He gave me words of warning. I looked back as I walked down the hill, as he walked away from me moving slowly, bent and grand.

47. Double Illumination

The atmosphere at Kozenji was not so different from the mood of our zendo half a world away. But these two places grew out of different Zen traditions, and like Protestantism and Catholicism, with respect to doctrine, articles of faith, and daily practice they have sometimes been opposed. After the road of the Buddhist tradition forked in Japan in the 13th century, in China in the ninth, in India long before, the paths grew further and further apart. "Many paths, one summit" is a new age cliché. Is it ecumenism? Multiculturalism? Transcendentalism? Whatever it is, it is not necessarily true.

"Not in this life," a Japanese Zen monk said. "Different summits. Or no summit."

Sakiyama spent his life breaking through koan after koan face to face with his teacher until he completed his arduous training, was certified a master and given approval to teach. His tradition, Rinzai Zen, was supported for centuries by the warrior elite of Japanese society.

A Zendo was founded in our town by monks who came to America from Antaiji Temple, a Zen temple near Kyoto, Japan. Anataiji was founded early in the 20th century by Sawaki Roshi. He wanted to create a temple that would emphasize seated meditation rather than rituals or scholarship as the central practice of spiritual life. He wanted a place where Zen monks could live a life of practice, and avoid the careerism that could easily override the spiritual aspirations of Japanese Zen monks. At this nearby Zendo, as at Antaiji, the practice method is simply to sit. Fold your legs this way, hands this way, tip of the tongue to the front of the palette, eyes cast down, spine tall, mind not sleeping, not thinking. That's it. What do you mean, that's it? I asked. What do we do? "Nothing" was the Japanese Zen monk's reply.

The thought "Total waste of time" crossed my mind.

"Yes." He surely would have agreed.

"Why do it?" (We did have this conversation.)

"No reason."

"But I see you make effort, many hours a day, you do long meditation retreats. You put a lot of effort into it. For no reason?"

"Yes."

"Why not watch TV for no reason? Why not just drink or be a criminal for no reason? They might describe what they do in the same words."

"They have a reason. A human reason. Zazen does nothing for a human reason."

Well this was unintelligible and useless to me. I thought: "Well, he is either deceiving me or he is playing some kind of word games or something." But I kept going back to the Zendo. Because his conviction was evident and seemed unshakable, his demeanor was peaceful, because the place was silent and serene.

Instead of working hard to grow an organization, to fundraise, to advertise, to increase membership, to charge a fee, to convince others of the special rightness of his way, as far as I could tell all he cared about was practice. Just doing it.

"People will like it or not like it," he said.

"But don't you have some obligation to offer it to them?"

"I do. They are welcome. But I don't want to pull them."

Well, I wanted kensho, an intense experience of realization. I heard about it. It was the point of Zen, as far as I knew.

"Don't worry about it. Just sit. Wholeheartedly."

"Wholeheartedly" was the fine print I missed. But I kept practicing.

After about 5 or 6 years of this mix of practice, confusion, tantalizing experiences, pain and speculation I came across a Tibetan tradition teacher who had studied in Dharamsala, with the Dalai Lama. Excellent... And he worked in the diamond business in New York. Excuse me? That does not sound like a Buddhist job. It did not match my prejudices about what a religious life was supposed to be. It did, however, sound pretty close to my own

experience… And he was a scholar, someone who could explain
what Buddhism was all about. I hoped that by listening to what he
had to say then maybe Zen would come clear. So I listened to what
he had to say. Instantly, I said yes, I want to know about this… that
sounds right… exactly…. In a week or two my mind opened, and
then again and again, as, through clearly articulated, understandable
explanations the gorgeous, complete world of Buddhist doctrine
opened, and kept opening, like an infinite rose. Am I exaggerating?
No. His talks were not confusing Zen style lectures. Those had been

frustrating and disturbing to me; presenting me with the inadequacy of my understanding, without deepening it. His gave me access to what I always needed but never knew where to find.

One technique used in Zen lectures is to create doubt. Doubt in what? Doubt in the adequacy of the rational mind's use of perception, language and logic to accurately apprehend reality. So, if you are confined in a monastery, in a pressure cooker atmosphere, with your mind pressed hard against an impenetrable koan, the doubt may suddenly coalesce, and the habitual mental constructs by means of which you have been fabricating the world you thought existed as a fixed and objective fact outside of you and independent of your mind all along, become in an instant evident, and you realize something breathtakingly fresh about the way the world exists.

But at first it just sounds confusing. Outside a full-time monastic training environment and without a basic education in Buddhist doctrine, lectures intended to prove the inadequacy of language fail in their objective. Instead of allowing people to understand that language is inadequate to capture the reality it is intended to describe, it makes them feel that they are personally inadequate. It makes them defensive and cliquey. They become emotionally needy and dependent on the judgments of the teacher. I had hoped for more from Zen teaching and practice. Now, like finding an oasis or reaching home, I had intelligent explanations of what Buddhism actually teaches.

I learned how to use the intellect to open the gates of wisdom. I had a key to the treasury of Buddhist literature. This understanding gave me faith in sitting in meditation. Now I could understand why it was essential to do this kind of practice every day; why it is true that zazen gives us our real life, beyond the human concerns of gain and loss.

Using the study of logic, perceptual analysis, cosmology, karma, metaphysics, and vowed morality I could proceed naturally to the zendo. Instead of being asked to obey, accept, remain willfully ignorant of doctrine, I was asked to think, understand, practice. This does not contradict Zen. It opens the door to Zen.

I had faith in karate practice too. I wanted to be like the people I saw doing it. I aimed at embodying the form even when I knew little about it.

On a trip to Okinawa, when I saw genuine advanced practice for the first time, I was stunned. I did not understand how they could move like that! Each technique powerful and precise, each person's body snapping from move to move like a whip. I had practiced karate for nine years at that time. I had traveled around the US to dojos and events in many styles, but I had never seen a human being move like those Okinawans did.

I thought maybe the Okinawans were born with it. I continued to practice the shallow karate I knew when I came back to the US. I sweated and I persevered. I thought about the miraculous movement I had seen back on Okinawa from time to time, but I did not dwell on it. I just practiced. I believed my practice would somehow go deeper and deeper. Somehow I would approach mastery, without my having to know how it all really worked. I hoped that devoted practice of the form would be enough.

When I returned to Okinawa the next time, seven years later, with 16 years of practice, what I saw the Okinawans do still looked miraculous, but my understanding was very different. The ground had been prepared by my years of effort and aspiration. This time I was able to imitate what they did. Moves that I had understood as a matter of leverage and straight lines of force were, as he executed them, high-speed whipping helices.

Until that time I had learned to emit energy by using my arms like pistons and the vertical axis of my spine like a camshaft. But this, I learned, produces only a tiny fraction of the speed and power that the human body is capable of. This dimension of karate practiced has not yet been widely studied in the West.

Long years of practice prepared me for sudden insight. The wall fell. For a long time I proceeded haltingly, not knowing what was ahead, with no map or way to find out. Now the way ahead was clear.

48. Door Number Two

The time came to build the dojo. None of us knew what we were doing. But we did not let that detail stand in our way. We turned up the music and leapt into action. The joint compound was two inches thick on the sheetrock where one of the guys' enthusiasm outran his knowledge.

Another guy was hand sawing 80 feet of edge off the top of sheet rock that somehow stuck up a little high above one wall. He was going at it for half an hour with only about 70 feet left to go when one of the electricians working in the space next door saw what he was up to and lent him his SawZall. Ten minutes later the job was done. A tall skinny kid was ramming the dull blade of a circular saw into a cut halfway into a sheet of plywood, ramming that baby home again and again, as the machine screeched and burned. Someone told him: You can replace the blades in those things. Oh.

And yes, some sections of the place looked like they were built by beavers. But once it was done the quality of the workmanship wasn't what you noticed.

For a few days we slept on the cold hard floor. We cleared the debris and trained karate when we were done with our work for the day.

Then my friends went home. And it was quiet. An empty room in a new town with a sign on the door that said, "karate." And the room in the back of a mill, hidden from the road, so far from Main Street that people still, after all these years, say I didn't know you guys were here. And there I was, looking out over the river, and practicing.

Once in a while someone would call. Wrong number. A supermarket has almost the same number as us with two of the digits reversed. I spoke to many dyslexics that first year. And: Do you have kickboxing? No, sorry. Tae Kwon Do? Ninjutsu? No. Once in a while someone would want to check out a class. But when they came in to watch there was no one in the class. So I talked to them and persuaded a few to try it out and soon there were a few people practicing. I taught three classes a day, six days a week. Most attended only by myself. Once in a while a student showed up. I had plenty of time to hone my skills.

Despite the lack of evidence I was convinced that what I was doing was a great thing. So I just kept on. People told their friends. The Ninja Turtles had offices next door, and kids and families and artists would wander over to the dojo, curious. I kept the heat down to save money. I slept here. I had nothing to offer but practice.

The first students that joined mattered very much to me. When they succeeded I was proud, when they quit I felt betrayed. Everything was personal. But so many people have come and gone. So many practitioners doing so well and then disappearing without notice. And ones you think you'll never see again keep coming back five, ten, twenty years later, day after day. All those hopes and heartbreaks burn, and then burn out, so you don't get so attached after a while. You just train.

49. Intelligent Body, Strong Mind

Our actions—what we do, say and think—change the quality and character of our lives. Small effects accumulate as we practice. Under pressure or in crisis what we have done is all we will have to depend on. People make the mistake of thinking they can depend on their talents, their credits, their knowledge, their connections, their possessions, their luck. Whatever we imagine, if we don't practice we will be unable to act decisively.

If you are living a life of practice you constantly refine and polish your body and mind in the heat and pressure of training. It changes not only what you can do, but how you are.

As you practice your mind connects with your body. Soon there is no gap between your intention and your action. You notice muscles in your feet, in your neck, along your spine, in your hands, muscles you never sensed before. And it's all you. You feel different. When I started training, getting to the floor to do pushups felt awkward, uncomfortable and slow. After a while you drop down, you spring back up, naturally, like a carp in a pond, your body snapping like a spring, moving instantly and effortlessly.

It happens that many of the slogans and explanations I heard as a beginner, which were inscrutable at first, became simple, clear descriptions of reality. Bring your energy up from the earth. Breathe through your center. Create flows of energy along such and such a pathway. At first it sounded like gibberish to me. The words corresponded to nothing that I could perceive.

After a while these words of advice focused my attention on natural processes I could—at first fleetingly, then more concretely—perceive.

The connective tissue of the body strengthens and begins to form a unified whole. Even the quality of the internal organs change.

Your mind changes. It stabilizes. Regulating your life with a practice schedule, regulating your body, breath, and thinking, brings your emotions also under your control. This does not mean that you repress them. It means your emotions are yours, they aren't things that happen to you. You can respond or not respond, use them or set them aside. This doesn't happen automatically, just because you punch and kick. But if you train properly, it happens.

Regulating your life means building into your schedule a pulse of pressure and release, hard work and rest. Completing the sine wave of training in the course of each day, until it becomes natural. This dynamic pulse is an essential characteristic of good training.

A punch has a compression and release phase. The muscles contract then they relax. As you practice you get faster, more precise and more powerful by learning to tighten and release various parts of the body, in sequence, at just the right time. Or you can sustain relaxation—in rest or meditation—and sustain tension—for isometric stamina training—for an extended period of time.

Exhilaration is part of it. Pain is too. Getting freaked out at discomfort or the prospect of discomfort is a very uncomfortable way to live, so this aspect is useful.

With training we can integrate the body and mind. Under the influence of modern life we tend to split the body and mind. A man comes into the dojo with his son. They are smart. They prize their intellects. They believe in the split between flesh and spirit. They sit at their computers. They drive in their car. They go to the movies. They sit and watch and think and talk. As smart as they are they assume they should mask their weaknesses and boast about their strengths. They came in hoping they might change. Perhaps they might become renaissance men, bridge the divide between scholar and warrior, soldier and statesman, jock and nerd.

Through practice your mind becomes stronger and your body becomes more intelligent.

50. Honest Action

How do you know how hard to train? How much to meditate? Take the example of a guitar string: If there is too little tension in it, it won't make any sound at all. Put too much tension in it and the string will break. It needs just the right amount of tension. And the optimal tension for each string is different. The same holds true for how much pressure each person should undergo in training.

People can get carried away by the energy of the group and get hurt. Some may float along, wasting their time. The teacher has to be tuned in to the capacity and motivation of each student to help them set the level that's right for them.

One day in August, when we have our testing for new ranks, a student was demonstrating her kata by herself in front of the whole group. This was part of her test for her green belt. All eyes were on her.

This woman had about a year's experience. Her movements were focused and sharp. She was a refined, sophisticated person, so it was especially jarring when, in the midst of her demonstration, there came a roaring sound from the hallway off the rear of the dojo where the bathrooms were. No one was sure quite what it was, but soon it was over and she continued. Then came another roar. This time it was the unmistakable sound of vomiting. The sound of a man overtaken by hearty full-throated heaves as he disgorged the contents of his stomach.

A look crossed this woman's face I have never seen before, and I hope will never see again. Terrified and grossed out at the same time. What the hell am I doing here? she wondered. But no. It was too late to ask. She was standing there in front of hundreds of strangers, sweating! punching!, while this guy blows his lunch in the next room—and no one seems to notice! What on earth am I doing here?

We felt sorry for her. Nervous titters. We felt sorry for him. But it was a hot and humid day and this guy had not been training very much lately. And today, on test day, when the place is crowded and the training is hard, he decides to ignore those facts and for ceremonial reasons, he shows up. And it was too much for him. His spirit was sort of willing but his flesh said no way. And what should we do about this? What is the traditional response to a guy vomiting down the hall during a test? Like a nose pick on view in a seventh grade math class or Holden Caulfield's fart in church, although people tried to keep it together in honor of the solemnity of the occasion there was no way to hold back the flood. Through clenched teeth giggles began around the room. Do we not all hear this? People are looking at each other, trying stoic calm. Do we pretend there's not a guy puking? It was a tense atmosphere to begin with, and of all the people to be interrupted by vomiting. She was so prim, so put together. Silence returned. She proceeded. Then came the roaring sound of this poor man's innards convulsing at a whole new level. We're approaching the Richter scale. Children noticed, got worried, giggled and covered their faces, people were embarrassed, a doctor and a nurse went back to see if they could help the man and the rest of us got on with the test. Stillness. It must be over, we're gonna be okay. She went on demonstrating her kata. No! It's not over. Low moans... More! Yes! But the guy trained for years after that and the lady never came back. The guitar string has to be tuned just right. Although sometimes when it isn't, you can still include the results as part of training.

On one visit to Okinawa I saw a demonstration in which one man tightened his body so completely that another was able to break a baseball bat over his arm, and a 2-by-4 over his back. I trained with them. The demonstration was no trick. They were strong.

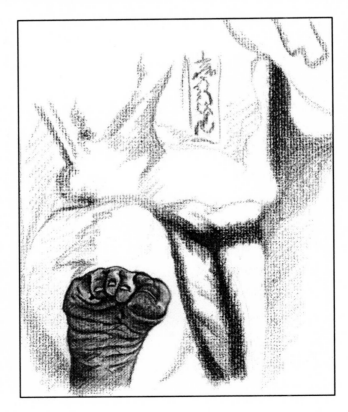

In the "Naihanchi" group of kata, the entire body undergoes high tension. The blood pressure increases. Even the bones get training effect. This training method helps to create a seamless sheath of energy, flowing along arches of muscle and bone from head to toe. To increase the pressure of training beyond the comfort level, the instructor will strike into the muscles of the practitioner. A knife hand strike or a toe tip kick to the big muscles of the arms, legs, back, abdomen, etc., brings the person to a heightened state of arousal, like the strike of the keisaku stick in the zendo. The strike puts your body on red-alert and requires that you dig deep down into your reserves of power. By going to the limit of our ability we come back after a day of rest, stronger, with more capacity than ever.

This training has to be done with skill. It takes precise knowledge of the structure of the body and its targets and of the individual you are training.

There were about thirty black belts and brown belts in the dojo one night and we were doing this kind of Naihanchi training for about half an hour or so everybody is sweating and working hard and I lay a powerful roundhouse kick into the abdomen of one of the black belts and the guy farts. This wasn't something you could over look. It was something so potentially famous and humiliating that even if we did see the guy again everyone would think about this every time they saw him. I didn't want that. He was a good guy. So rather than over look it I announced: "One honest fart is better than a thousand phony punches. Hit! Hit! Hit!" And that was that.

We cannot hide from embarrassment, from our bodies, from our limits, from our mortality. I lead a meditation group in the jail. I don't go only for the sake of people in there. I also go because those guys are coming out. Prisons and hospitals collect suffering. Unless we make a special effort to transform suffering into something else, suffering will continue and it will spread. Most of the time we don't think about prisons and hospitals. We don't give much thought to the fact of suffering in our own lives, until we are forced by circumstances to face it. Human beings feel shame and fear. For the millions locked in prison the feeling is more intense. As for hospitals: all of us, and everyone we know, will face illness, old age, and death. The more completely we try to exclude unpleasantness from our lives the more effort it takes, and the more alienated we become from the reality of our own lives. Peace will escape us, and we will not see why. Training demands that we face all aspects of our lives squarely.

Nothing extra. Nothing missing. Everything included.

51. Kurosawa's Craft

In the Japanese film "The Seven Samurai" a village is under siege by a murderous gang. For the villagers it's humiliation now and death soon. Something must be done. Two villagers travel to town to hire a samurai, a professional soldier, to defend their village. After a search they find one who may be willing. But… he will need some more men. All the villagers have to offer as payment is a handful of rice. These are hard times. Unemployed samurai are everywhere. The samurai sees the villagers' desperation. As a professional warrior it is his moral obligation to serve. His existence is meaningless except in service to others. Even these extremely humble masters qualify. He accepts their offer.

He gets right to work. First task: recruiting the right candidates for his small army. To succeed against the long odds his men will need to be good. How to test them?

He has a plan. He sits inside the doorway of a storefront, visible from the busy street. He stations his young assistant just inside the doorway where the assistant could attack anyone entering from the street into the storefront. The head samurai sits in the center of the room, looking out toward the street. He gestures to a young tough looking samurai, who happens to be walking down the street, to come in. The young man comes in. As he crosses the threshold the hidden assistant hits him over the head with a wooden sword. The young samurai flails his arms, curses them both and departs. The leader sits back down.

When he sees another likely candidate passing by outside he calls out to him. This one is slightly better dressed than the first, and stronger looking, too. The second fellow crosses the threshold, but he reacts instantly. Before the blow from the assistant can land the second fellow parries the attack. He stomps off, angrily. The leader shakes his head and waits.

He sees another samurai coming along. This one has an intelligent, dignified bearing. The leader gestures to him to come in. This samurai takes a few steps toward the doorway and stops, before even reaching the threshold. A smile crosses his face, and he gestures toward the guy hiding—unseen by him but detected nevertheless— as if to say hey, what's the story? Smiling, the leader calls the hiding guy out in the open and invites this razor sharp samurai to join their force, without ever seeing him so much as unsheathe his sword.

Where is your mind when you face an opponent? If it is on your technique you will respond mechanically. You will be too slow. If your mind alights on a target on his body you will be striking where he was, not where he is. If you think at all you will either anticipate or hesitate. You will get stuck a second in the past or a second in the future. You have to drop your thought and freely respond to the situation as it evolves. You cannot behave spontaneously without rigorous training because your mind will be disturbed, and your body will not respond skillfully to your will. An untrained person, in a moment of pressure will plan or freeze with dread, go wild or collapse.

To respond skillfully in the moment of action you must be beyond thought. It is not mystical. Any athlete, pilot, musician, warrior or Zen master relies on it.

After a while, through training, it becomes natural to be beyond thought when faced with an opponent. Access to that state of mind, called hishiryo in Japanese, becomes second nature. That is as far as most accomplished martial artists get. But it is only the second example in the story above. There is a level of development beyond it. You can't skip to it. You have to move into the second stage, and habituate to it, before you can move beyond it.

What characterizes the example of the third samurai is loss of attachment to his subjective view. At that level when an opponent appears you are not limited by your own perspective. You sense your opponent's characteristics, the environment, the unseen potentiality of the whole setting. The second samurai in the story, as skillful as he was, was depending on his own training and his own strength as he walked through the threshold. He was preoccupied with a view of the world in which he was at center stage, in which the rest of the world was the cast and scenery. That limited the range of possibilities for his own action.

In fact it distorted his view of reality. He is not the leading actor "in reality" from anyone's point of view but his own. Seeing from everyone's point of view at once would be impossible, unless it is done beyond thought. You can't skip to it. It can only be done through intensive, deliberate, well-informed training.

This serves not just in self-defense but in every situation. This is the action free from ignorance, free from hindrance.

52. Forging Body & Mind

The words "Oku Myo Zai Ren Shin" are embroidered on the black belts in our school. "Deeply hidden reality arises through the transformation of the heart and mind in training." The word "Ren" means transformation. The same character appears in the Japanese word for alchemy: Ren Kin Jutsu, literally "the art of transforming gold." The Chinese character Ren includes a radical that represents iron, and Ren represents the process of pounding the iron, as you would if you were shaping a samurai sword. That pounding changes not only the shape of the metal but its quality as well.

The swordsmith heats the iron until it's red-hot. He pulls the iron from the coals and places it on the anvil. Striking at just the right places, with just the right intensity, he hammers the short, thick, hard block of metal into the shape of a sword blade.

He then begins folding the metal. Again and again he heats the metal shaft until it is glowing red. With his hammer he folds it in half along the length of the piece, cools it in a bucket of water, heats it, and then folds it in half again. Soon there are thousands of fine, laminated layers of steel, making a blade far stronger and more flexible than the crude, brittle block of iron it was made from.

At each heating the steel has to reach a precise temperature, 1350 degrees centigrade. Hot enough to work, cool enough to exclude impurities. Analysis of the crystalline structure of the steel done with modern metallurgical measurement shows that the finest Japanese sword makers could accurately judge the temperature of the glowing steel they were working to within one degree. That was centuries before the thermometer was invented.

After each round of hammering the hot blade was plunged into water to cool it. The cooling helped create the precise crystalline structure and bonding that made the medieval Japanese sword the most advanced metallurgy before the modern age. According to a once secret manual, the water in which the blade was cooled needed to be "the temperature of a lake in February or August." If the metal cooled too rapidly or too slowly it would not have the properties necessary to cut through armor, to pierce bone, slash through the wooden shafts of spears and halberds, or break an enemy's blade, while remaining unharmed. Lives depended on the quality of the transformation of that steel.

The precise judgments made again and again changed the metal, but also the people who worked it. The transfer of knowledge, taught, demonstrated and copied, from generation to generation, bound not only the layers of pure steel, but the lives of those people and the integrity of that transmission. Look at that swordsmith. Look at his face when he is working, his hands, his body. Look at the apprentice assisting him. It is not only the metal that changes. Real karate is like that, for teachers and students.

That is the "Ren" which is written on our belts and diplomas, and which manifests in our bodies and minds. That kind of transformation is what practice ought to entail. Our bodies and minds are the material of our own art. We need that precision, that intensity, and that ceaseless repetition aimed at perfection.

As we undergo this process of transformation our understanding of perfection itself will be transformed. How? From the pursuit of perfection as an imaginary ideal which we presume to have a fixed set of qualities which we label as "perfect." An ideal we assume to be out there somewhere, in the future, in another place. To an intimate and direct perception that our universe is all perfect, and always will be. We cannot assert this and have it be true. It would be a lie and a fantasy to say "It's all perfect now," so I'll just drift through life, and pretend all the crap I have to deal with everyday doesn't really exist. It won't work. It won't be true. You would suffer from pretending it was. But, when the time is right, and your transformation is complete, then the evidence will be indisputable and the assertion will be utterly true. Your suffering will be over.

53. Maximum Killing Power

In some situations an unarmed person may have an advantage over an armed attacker. Against a person armed with a holstered gun, or someone standing next to you reaching for a knife, you would have an advantage, if you were trained, for a fraction of a second.

In the scene from the movie *Indiana Jones And The Raiders Of The Lost Ark* where Harrison Ford draws his gun and shoots the threatening sword master, command of technology trumped virtuoso skill. If we isolate the result—Indiana beats the swordsman—it looks like technology gives an out and out advantage. But look at it from the causal direction—the choices leading up to the confrontation—and you get a very different picture. Since the quality of the body and mind of a practitioner changes as he masters his art, it's not just the magnitude of his effect on the world that changes, the quality of his effect changes too.

In traditional practice the heart and mind are cultivated as we strengthen the body. Increases in power that come from technological change insidiously cut us off from the world and damage the world we think we are mastering. Picking up a gun at first feels like an out and out increase in power. If you are in a confrontation you would have an advantage in power. But watch what happens when an untrained person carries a weapon. His mind changes, and not in the way a practitioner's does. The mind narrows its range of concern. It more narrowly defines what is relevant and, because the technology commands so much of our limited mental attention, restricts our engagement with the possibilities of life. A minus will accompany the increase in power. For an untrained person an increase in power comes with a decreased connection with the rest of the world.

Guns can be used as a means of training as certainly as swords or staffs or empty hands. The essay "Zen in the Art of Archery" was one of the books on the desk of my sixth grade teacher. It was one of the first essays on Zen by a westerner, (German author Eugen Herrigel), published in the west. It recounts the experience of the author in Japan just after World War II, as he learned traditional archery from a Japanese master.

In his book the author talks about shooting in a state of mind beyond thought, beyond the conscious intention to shoot. He tries to convey the transformation effected by consistent and rigorous training. He describes the way in which the sense of separation between the archer, the target and the act of shooting is supposed to vanish. Kyudo, the way of archery, is a method by which it is possible to eliminate mental disturbance, to see the mind in action as it splits unified reality into subject/object/action. Ultimately it is a method to deepen our connection with the world, to understand it, to live wholeheartedly in it, to realize its nature, and be free of suffering. That can be done using a gun as well as a bow an arrow. With this we can we can overcome our mistaken view of subjects and objects and beat swords into plowshares.

54. From the Shadows

Our black belt training runs late into the night, and we often train outdoors. Our training area is the wide sloping parking lot outside the dojo. If you walk beside the line of boulders that border the lot above the riverbank, walking downstream a few hundred feet, you will find a narrow path that squeezes past the building, close to the river. Beyond that is a bar. You can't see the entrance from where we train, but late at night in the summer you can hear voices and engines from over there.

One night someone appeared from the shadows. The path there is littered with junked equipment, pieces of fence, crumbled bricks and wood. Next to it there is a ten-foot sheer drop, down a concrete retaining wall. It used to house the mill wheel, but now there's nothing there. That night the trees blocked the moonlight. But in the shadows we could see someone standing still, watching us.

Twenty people dressed in black moving in unison in silence, stopping for a moment and then starting, simultaneously, again and again.

I approached the man. He was 6'5" at least. He had long hair, and a thick light colored mustache. He looked like a guy from a country rock band who'd been on the road way too long. He said, "Can I watch?" I said, "Sure." He then asked, "Can I join in?" I said, "Well you ought to sign up first." I was facing him, my back to the group, the members continuing their training. I noticed the knife on his belt. The knife must have been a foot long, part commando, part Bowie. I said, "Do you want to sign up now?" He said, "Yes, sir, I do."

I thought he would say he just wanted to watch and then be gone in a minute. But there he was following me up the stairs, him and his knife, and now his girlfriend was coming along too. She had been there in the shadows, waiting to see how it would all turn out. We went inside, and he did join, right then and there. Turns out he was a black belt in another style, just moved to the area, working and going to college. I never saw the knife again.

55. Doing Right

One of the members of the dojo brings dozens and dozens
of Christmas presents to people around town on Christmas Eve.
The only time he has ever missed training was to go to a wake or
a funeral or to visit someone in the hospital. If he sees something
useful he thinks someone might want he puts it in the back of his
truck and delivers it. He has gotten hurt but never complained.
Each year he goes to the biker rally at Sturgis, South Dakota. He
has barbed wire tattooed around his biceps. He was a Marine. He
says he always fought a lot. "Fought about what?" I asked. "Stupid
things," he replied. "Always stupid things."

His father was in a concentration camp in Poland. He wasn't a
Jew, but still he had it pretty bad, he said. He came over here and
he was poor when he grew up, so he held on to every penny, you
didn't waste nothing. He got to be very fat. It got to the point where
he couldn't work. He made his sons eat everything on the plate so
as not to waste it. The old man was rough with this son, all his sons,
yelling a lot. He kept the boys working all the time. They had it
rough growing up in the old country so the old man made it rough
on the boys, here. But, the way this guy sees it, it made him stronger.
He could do anything, he tells me. He could live anywhere.

In the dojo he feels the fire he felt in fights. He likes to work out
and run and lift weights. He trains hard. He runs every morning. In
the summer he sees his neighbors sitting on the porch drinking beer
when he comes home from work late on a Friday night. And when
he goes out for his 4:30 a.m. run on Saturday morning, he can see
them sitting there, still drinking. They think he's crazy to be so busy.

The things he fought about, when he thinks back and goes down the list, sure a lot of them were stupid things, but they were all about protecting people. One time they had to go to Fort Benning (an Army base) for jump school, because the Marines didn't have their own. That meant the Marines were hanging out with the soldiers. Even if it was Force Recon with Green Berets and Airborne Rangers it was still Marine and Army, and there was no doubt which side of the line you were on. He was having a talk with a Ranger. Nice guy. Across the room he saw this other Marine, a jerk, busting on some Green Berets: "Army sucks. Marines kick ass." That kind of stuff. Stupid stuff. He says to the Ranger, the nice guy, "You know if that jerk starts a fight over there I have to jump in and defend him. Honor of the corps." The Ranger says, "Yeah, I know."

And sure enough all hell broke loose. Fists, bottles, everyone going at it. Lots of damage. The guys had to pay for it. It took a long time to cover it on military pay. "Stupid stuff," he said.

Back home, he and some of his friends were at a karaoke night. This girl they used to know from school was there. She had a heart murmur, and she was a really bad singer. When she would get up to sing the guys would make fun of her. And she was handicapped and just trying to have a little fun. He was just back from the service. When he told those guys to shut their mouths, that she had more guts than they ever would to get up there and sing and they should leave her alone, they did stop. They left her alone after that. And they all had a really nice time.

He was always the one to break things up. And there was always something to break up, wherever he was. At Sturgis, Bike Week, with thousands of bikers showing their colors, these college kids pushed on this guy's Harley, nearly got themselves killed, would have, if he hadn't stepped in and calmed things down...

But he doesn't put on a show about it. Like Superman. Just soft spoken, at ease, look you right in the eye and see how you're doing. And giving out all those presents at Christmas.

56. Impermanence

What we call objects are events unfolding in slow motion. We assume things have fixed qualities. We think the qualities of some objects will make us happy. We do harmful things to obtain them and harmful things to keep them. And it doesn't make us happy.

We think we are a certain type. Some people say: I am the type nothing good ever happens to. That's just the way life is. Somebody else may have a high status job, a gorgeous face, an unreturnable tennis serve, a million bucks. These people may act as if those qualities are fixed. Innate. Dependable.

From a distance, viewing others, it is easy to see how silly that is. The depressed guy at the bar could pull himself up by his bootstraps, put down the glass, learn a trade and move on. The corporate vice president can get downsized, the fashion model will get old and wrinkly, a million bucks can disappear in a day.

Here is a danger practitioners may face: thinking they have certain fixed qualities. The mistake leads insecure people to think they will never get what they lack, and makes some good athletes complacent, so their effort, and skills, decline. Nothing is permanent.

We can have the lives we want because our qualities are not fixed. What we do determines our qualities.

A concert is not an object. It's an event. A storm is not an object. Who would think so? But when it comes to understanding physical phenomena and people we do make this mistake. They are not fixed 'things.' At some time in the past they didn't exist; then they came into existence when the causes and conditions were right. Someday, as those conditions shift, the person or the thing will cease to exist.

We overlook the vast concatenation of causes that produce every rock, tree, car, person, mountain, or galaxy, which are underway at every moment. We then label the thing we perceive, and our mind, as an energy-saving convenience, takes the label as representing a static thing with fixed qualities.

In karate training there are no things. There is nothing you 'have'. All there is is your action. What you know, what you once did, what you intend to do, only matter to the degree that they are manifest now. Your life is what you do, informed by habit, alive now in your motivation and your method. The rest is a fantasy.

Imagine an ocean. The beach there was once a battleground. On that beach is a memorial for the dead. On another beach are people on their summer vacation. Look at the ocean from these beaches. Does the ocean look different, or the same? The appearance changes as the condition of your mind changes.

Look at one wave. Let's say you wanted to see the ocean all your life but you lived far away from it, and you never had a chance. You heard about oceans, about the waves rolling in. And let's say you are old and your eyesight is fading, you have the wish to see the ocean one time before you die. Out of kindness your family brings you to the beach and a split second before your eyesight blinks out for the very last time you glimpse the ocean for an instant. You see this one great wave rising up, wild, foam flying, about to crash on the beach. You remember that wave. You know you will never forget it. You name it in your memory. That Wave. When you looked at the ocean, that's what you saw. There were, however, other people on the beach that day. People who had lived on the ocean all their lives. People spending their summer there. They walked on the beach every morning. They hardly noticed the waves anymore, never mind taking special note of one particular, unremarkable wave. They were there when That Wave came in. To you it was singular. It had qualities and characteristics, its own nature, a label you gave it, to distinguish it from all other waves, from everything else. To the strollers on the beach, however, it was another anonymous stirring of the water, produced by motion, preceded rhythmically by a previous wave, followed by a subsequent wave, endlessly, and more or less, without variation, without any significance at all.

That's the way it is with your first students. Each one is big, important, unique. That's why you give them so much, and why there's so much emotion in it when you make mistakes, and so rewarding when one flourishes. After a while it's not like that. If you have the chance to work with hundreds or thousands of people, your sense of them changes. You see them not especially as 'yours' but as people. Their bodies respond to the demands of training in ways you can predict. They will face difficulties you can anticipate. You can guide them through training because the structure of human lives is similar and you have done this many times before. It makes the process work, work smoothly, and you get good results more often.

But if your perspective on your students is just a pull back from close up to wide angle, then your perspective is still just a fragment of the truth, even if it is a bigger fragment. You go from seeing only those first few unique precious students to just seeing an ocean of undifferentiated people, appearing one after the next. That is a point when some teachers burn out and quit. But there can be another step. It is the natural result of continuing, if you keep caring, and shift your ambition from becoming a successful teacher to helping the students. There does come a point where you can see the uniqueness and value of each person, and at the same time see them in context as well.

The attachment that you feel to your first students, or your first love, makes them one of a kind. Teenagers feel that their group of friends is unique. Painfully or easily these attachments change. After you have taught a hundred students or a thousand students the feeling of attachment changes. You still understand each one, and you care about each one. We proceed from seeing one, to seeing a group, to seeing many individually. That is how a teacher matures.

As a teacher you should not conclude from the fact that you are deeply attached to the "first" and less so later, that you would be better off being non-attached to the first. You need that commitment to launch the process of transformation—for both student and teacher. The process of transformation begins by burning off the crude stuff. If we don't go through the first step the next and the next ten thousand, will not work.

For an advanced practitioner every relationship, every action and every moment can be fresh. It takes experience to see that it is always the first time that we have the moment we are in. That is beginner's mind.

A monk said to Zen Master Joshu:
"The many return to the one.
To what does the one return?"

57. The Sign

I return to the dojo to train each day and as I enter I see
something no one else sees. The wooden sign next to the door. Of
course everyone who enters sees the sign. But they don't see what I
see. It is a slab of pine three inches thick, three feet high, with one
side milled straight and the other following the rough contour of the
tree, two feet wide where it is widest.

My wife and I were married at the edge of the pond where the
Mill River slows and rises. There, where the Tibetan monks built
their beautiful sand mandala and blew the grains of sand into the
water, we were married. The Tibetans say that now, since that
mandala ceremony was held there, ten thousand buddhas inhabit the
pond. I think so.

It was a few years later when my wife carved the wooden sign
for the dojo door by hand. Tapping lightly on chisels for days. She
was not able to practice karate for a while at that time. She had been
training for years by then. Her training made her strong.

Years before, when she was mired in difficulty and her friends
told her to try karate, that it was just the thing. She gave it a try. And
it worked. Health and courage. Peace and action. What her friends
said would happen, happened.

Then one day she was working on a ladder two stories above a
marble floor when the ladder slid away from the wall. The doctors
said she was lucky. Doctors have a special view of luck. She could

not move well but she could hold a hammer and chisel, so there came the sign. That is how she continued to practice, that week.

When I see the wooden sign outside the front door, each day as I return to the dojo I cannot help but be touched by the way in which she and sincere people everywhere can continually take the pain of their lives and not pass it on, but instead transmute it into generosity and joy.

58. The Bell

The inclination to transmute pain to joy may come naturally but the ability to do it requires training. Physical training alone will not do it. I have a few meditation cushions to sit on. For a few hours a week the dojo became a zendo, a quiet place to meditate on a regular schedule.

Several people joined in right away. Two had known each other for years. They had crossed paths at retreats and other sitting groups in the area. Both had confusing, frustrating experiences. It had happened several times: they would meet a 'teacher' who would tell them, for example, to 'take vows'. Without knowing what they were saying or what they were supposed to get out of it they were asked to go through a ceremony in a language they did not understand, mimicking the words, and hoping for the best. Both felt disappointed, encountering in Buddhism the same kind of magical thinking and hollow ritual they had rejected in the religions in which they'd grown up.

When a famous Zen teacher visited the area to hold a Zen retreat one asked the teacher "What do we do?" He was asking the teacher how to meditate. The teacher said nothing. In the face to face interview part of Zen training the student is instructed to begin the interview by announcing what their practice is. But they did not know. So they asked the teacher "What is our practice?" The teacher repeated "What is your practice?" For a while they thought their confusion was their own fault.

The early Zen masters in China and Japan were well educated in the fundamentals of Buddhist doctrine, and well grounded in the literature. As they lived a life of practice and study they went beyond the limitations of intellect. Their practice was powerful. They understood the ideas upon which their practice was based, saw with their own eyes and felt with their own heart the example of people who had practiced sincerely for decades and, as a result, had total faith in what they were practicing. Because they had studied, listened and observed their teachers they understood in detail the ways in which an impulsive, untrained mind is easily deceived and how this leads to suffering.

They understood—by observation of the example of others, and soon by their own experience—the way that practice would lead them out of suffering. They understood the means. And they knew something about the results they could expect.

Many modern practitioners ignore this. And their practice fails because of it. Without understanding this "faith in practice" is nothing more than hoping for the best. A student-teacher relationship will not flourish just because you get a membership at a center and pay your dues. That is like a religious blind date. Unless the student and the teacher enter a relationship, gradually, with knowledge, with a close observation of the other person over time, an informed, honest and deeply trusting connection between the two—the basis of effective practice—will not form. It takes both self-confidence and mutual respect every step of the way. Emotional dependence on the part of the student and arrogance on the part of the teacher will cause the relationship to fail, and the practice of both will be nothing more than wasted effort.

59. First, Be Not a Jerk

One time we were in the midst of preparation for Jukai—the ceremony in which people take vows of moral and ethical conduct. For a year and a half the members of the meditation group studied a curriculum of subjects in Buddhist history and basic doctrine, Zen practice, and vows. On this particular evening I was talking about the three trainings that comprise Buddhist practice. The three trainings are in moral conduct, meditation, and wisdom.

We were discussing the teachings on morality, which are central to the taking of vows, and to leading a good life. Almost half of the books of Buddhist canonical literature are concerned with this subject. Among the vows we were preparing to take were the vows not to kill, not to steal, not to lie, not to use intoxicants, not to engage in sexual misconduct.

The premise on which the vow-taking is based is that the happiness of one's life and of all one's relationships is based on the quality of one's own actions. The result of keeping one's vows is a more peaceful mind and a happier life. We discussed the way karma works by carefully looking at the way the reality of our lives will shift based on our own actions and mental condition.

The subject of that evening's talk was the idea that Buddhism prescribes the observance of a strict code of moral and ethical conduct as a pre-requisite for a good life. One fellow who was there that night had been coming to the group regularly for a few months. He stood out from the rest of the regular visitors. He wore robes from the Catskill Zen center I had visited years before. Week after week he sat during the discussion stiffly staring. The other people—from college students to retirees, beginners and experienced practitioners—were all interested in the discussion and happy to be there. But as I was talking about the fact that kindness and self-restraint are necessary to put an end to suffering, this guy turns red and says furiously "In all my thirty years of Zen I have never heard anyone mention morality!" And he stormed out of the room.

He hadn't heard it before. Some of the Buddhist teachers who came to the U.S. in the sixties knew they were teaching young hippies, who wanted to hear about 'spontaneity,' not self-restraint. So this man, for thirty years, missed the essential teachings of Buddhism. Now the time had come when we could practice real Buddhism, not the hippie jumble that had wasted the time of so many well-meaning people.

That day the 30-year Zen practitioner finally heard about morality. One day we all do. Whether good conduct is expressed in the Ten Commandments, in the Seven Deadly Sins, the Bodhisattva Vows or in the pratimoksha instructions for monks, they all encourage us to treat others well, and to use our body and mind not as toys, but as the means to put an end to suffering.

Some people deny the truth of this. They say, "Just do what feels good… Don't censor your impulses… Get out your aggression…" They will tell you that sophistication is all about indulging your desires and refining your appetites…. They end up doing harm and losing their lives.

This is hard for some people to see because to them licentiousness looks like freedom. Look at any gambler, drug addict, smoker, drunk or pornographer and you can see how self-indulgence will enslave you. But we don't necessarily see this on our own. It requires study to see it and training to live it.

60. The Myth of the Privileged Frame

Let's say you toss a diamond out of the window of your car while traveling down the highway through the desert at 90 miles and hour. Someone sitting in the back seat of the car sees that diamond whiz backwards past them. The diamond *is* going backwards. Let's say a hitchhiker is standing at the side of the road. He sees you toss the diamond. He sees the diamond going forward, although not quite as fast as the car. The diamond *is* going forward. Which one is true? Forward or backward? It can't go forward and backward at the same time. Yes, it can. From multiple perspectives, each is true and both are true. Each person has their own frame of reference within which their observation is true. But reality has no single privileged frame of reference.

If you are the surveyor building that road through the desert you will mark the sides of the road as parallel lines stretching as far as the road will go. The road will always be the same width, to the inch. Wherever you are you could take a measurement at a right angle to one side of the road and find the other side of the road an equal distance away. Parallel lines will never converge. Your job, and the safety of all the travelers on that road, depend on the truth of this fact.

Then let's say you finish your summer job as a surveyor for the road company and go back to the astrophysics department to continue your classes. At a certain distance from earth we don't talk about space—how far away a certain planet is - we speak in terms of time - how many billions of years the light from that region has traveled to get to us. If you travel through the universe straight lines bend, time shifts, and all things are in motion. Parallel lines converge or diverge. The universe will not exist, and your Ph.D. will not be awarded, if you fail to understand this.

You always wake up in the same place you went to sleep. No surprise there. But the earth spun at a thousand miles an hour all night, that's 8,000 miles you've traveled (if you get your eight hours of sleep), every night of your life, and what's more our galaxy flew 660,000 miles every hour out toward infinity. And yet, here we are.

In Buddhism we are taught that the cause of suffering is ignorance. The cause is not chance. The cause of suffering is not the bad acts of other people. Ignorance. But ignorance of a particular kind: we believe what we perceive to be *the* truth is the total truth. In fact until we have completed our practice ours is a fragmentary, relative truth that is limited by our perspective. We mistakenly believe we have the whole picture. We act on that mistaken belief. In light of that how surprising is it that we do not get the result we hoped for?

Let's say you are sitting on the beach as the sun is going down. Many people are there, up and down the beach. The sunlight is glinting off the water. Golden flashes are visible to everyone. In general. But the glint you see is a reflection of a ray of sunlight from a particular facet on the surface of the water. The sunlight falls evenly on the water. And it is reflected from every point on the surface. But the beam that shines at the precise angle so that it hits your particular eye at a particular moment, is unique. And it has no existence as a 'glint' until it is seen. There are endless rays bouncing off the surface of the water. A glint, that you see, is made of the sunlight, and your perception of it. No perception, no phenomenon, no 'glint'.

Putting an end to our ignorance puts an end to our suffering. When we can see from our own perspective and that of others simultaneously our compassion deepens, our wisdom deepens, our ability to help ourselves and others deepens, and suffering comes to an end. With precise and diligent practice it can be done.

61. Sakiyama's Letter

Enkakuji Temple in Kamakura, Japan holds a special retreat once a year called a kojirin sesshin, a special time set aside from the regular monastery schedule when the temple is open not just to monks but to anyone who wants to come. For many years there was only one ordained priest visiting the temple for that retreat. It was a powerful Okinawan karate master who attended the retreat each year with a group of his students. The monk was Sakiyama Roshi. When I met him he was in his mid 70s and was no longer practicing karate actively. But he urgently communicated his understanding of karate and Zen to me.

He said:

"Today many karate students, particularly karate teachers, neither know the difference between karate and karate-do, nor do they try to discover the difference. This I regret very much. True karate-do can be learned only when we have realized the mysteries of our heart and mind, and realized the mysteries of our body with all our heart and mind and strength. Otherwise karate will be nothing more than a little game, a way to show off. Ultimately it will degenerate into contests or street fighting. It is a shame.

"The essentials of karate-do can only be attained through profound practice. This means that in order to realize what is essential we must experience deep meditation. I am sure you fully understand what I am trying to say. It is most important for us, and for the younger generations, that we cultivate our heart and mind.

"The final hurdle for us is to be free from the limitations of our own ego. The disease of modern people is that they are slaves to money, power, fame, etc. They are enslaved by their own egos, and are unaware of it. You will become a true master when you become aware of it, and become free of it. There is no easy way, but it is the most important task, one worth devoting one's life to accomplishing. This is the central task for anyone trying to master a true martial art.

"As I am writing to you I can vividly feel your sincerity and passion to pursue this and to master karate-do. 'Do' is an endless and severe way. Therefore we must endlessly exert ourselves to attain it. How wonderful the 'Do' is!"

No book or tape, no class or group membership, could do what he did for me. Sakiyama Roshi was able to see from many perspectives at once. He described our encounter in Okinawa an 'en'—a precise set of conditions all coming together at just the precise moment. He described the arrival of his package and at the precise moment I needed it also as an 'en'. The underlying conditions that allowed his words and actions to have their sudden effect on me were present because of years of practice, his and mine, and that of countless others.

62. Beyond the Art of the Deal

Among the unintended consequences of modern commercial culture is the habit of turning human relationships into deals. We do it in the name of fairness. Fairness is better than unfairness. But it is a degraded basis for human relationships and it doesn't work in a dojo. If you have a marriage where each person insists on only doing 50 percent, the marriage will be unhappy. Its not my hour to baby sit, or you didn't come up with your percentage of the electric bill. The bickering would be endless and eventually the baby will be unwatched and the lights will go out and the effort spent on settling grievances would exhaust the couple. If each person is committed to doing 100 percent, then the marriage will be happy. Each person can totally rely on the other, no matter what. It's a wonderful feeling. But if one person is committed to the 100 percent and the other to something less, then there will be exploitation and unhappiness. So what really works is everyone giving everything they can. That is the opposite of what we learn in the marketplace. In a store, in a deal, in a contract, in a negotiation, we seek to give the least and get the most. This may create an efficient distribution of scare resources, but kindness and generosity are not scarce resources. It is possible to produce them endlessly.

Stinginess and mistrust cannot be carried over into dojo life, if the dojo is going to function as a place of liberation. Each person has to understand that by giving the most they get the most. If we go all-out in our training we get as strong as possible. If we hold back we don't. If we seek out opportunities to help others learn, we benefit by having a chance to shift perspective, and by making the effort to analyze and convey the karate techniques properly, we gain deeper insight into them ourselves. We also build the habit of leading based on taking responsibility for the achievement of others. We will not get these benefits by being stingy with our time or energy or by remaining alone and unchallenged.

Money is important to people, so in the dojo we keep it very simple. No fundraising, no special fees, no founder's birthday donations, no seminars, no goods for sale, no extras, no shakedowns, no surprises. And not free. You pay your membership dues. There is no limit on what you get back. Because people pay something they value what they get. Usually teachers of free community center, garage and basement classes quit teaching after a short time. It is good to be generous with your time and money. However, you will not be helping people if you exhaust yourself without appreciation and mutual support.

If everyone pitches in then everyone in the dojo has a forum in which to be generous and to work their hardest. Nobody feels cheated or taken advantage of.

We are so accustomed to giving the least and getting the most, so on guard against being taken advantage of, that we may also forget that commerce can be good. A free and fair exchange of value benefits both parties. If you have grain and need cloth, and you meet someone who has cloth and needs grain and you trade, it's good. If there is coercion, greed or deception driving the exchange, it is not good.

The model for relationships in the dojo sometimes gets people thinking about the other relationships in their lives. One dojo member felt he was being treated unfairly at work. He walked away from the job one day and the next week they called him, and hired him back for more pay.

One woman, a beginner, came to class and cried all the way through. She did every move well, never daydreamed or wobbled, but through the warm-ups, the basics, the kata practice, tears poured down. As she was leaving I said: "Hey, what's wrong?" She just shook her head. For the first time in her life, at home, when a slap was coming toward her, she backed up out of the way instead of freezing in place. That did it. All hell broke loose. She was out of there. Did karate practice give her that ability? Did being part of a group of strong people? She had joined only a month before because she wanted to be able to defend herself.

63. The Threshold

I picked some patio blocks from a pallet in the yard at a building supply company. The guy asked me what I was going to use them for and I said for breaking. Breaking? With your hand? Yes, with my hand. He said, break these with your hand and I'll give you new ones free. So I spanned the two patio blocks across a pair of cinder blocks and broke them. I got the free ones. I saved two bucks.

In the dojo we break a brick or two as part of the black belt test. When it comes time for the prospective black belts to break their bricks, they are highly pumped up. They accept the risk of breaking their hand, and they go for it. Very few break their hand. Most break the bricks. They surprise themselves with their power. It's a satisfying feeling, the cement splitting and then nothing there but air. It isn't difficult if you are prepared. However if you are unprepared it's impossible.

All the conditions have to be in place in order for the break to work. Correct technique, a conditioned body, a focused mind, the ability to put power precisely into the target. It takes years. If the conditions are in place, the decisive moment comes naturally— protecting your life, breaking the brick, realization, falling in love.

64. Grasping

We are subject to many influences that get in the way of practice. If we succumb to them we are hurt. If we are aware of them it is possible to create good conditions for our practice.

It is difficult to restrain technology. The engine that drives a story, a culture or a life also drives the spread of technology. That engine is desire: what people want.

One technology wizard was asked about how he decides what projects to pursue. Market research? Focus groups? Laboratory breakthroughs? He said, "I lay in bed at night and think about what sucks." The man has made billions by getting people what they want. If a technology gives us the means to attain objects or feelings we think will make us happy, the technology will be discovered and deployed. That is what has propelled the history of technology.

Technology would only be morally neutral if it were unconnected to human minds. It is intimately connected. It is an expression of human mind. Modern culture makes people lonely. Because of technological and cultural solutions that seem to offer happiness we have developed a kind of cultural autism: we sit alone in cars. We sit in separate rooms watching separate channels on TV. We sit in separate cubicles working intimately with computers and other machines. We seek solace for our loneliness through machines and chemicals.

We misunderstand the source of our suffering and prescribe the wrong medicine to remedy our condition. The technology available to us can have a poisonous effect because it provides a way to exaggerate poisonous states of mind.

Being isolated makes you weak and vulnerable. Being connected makes you stronger and more able. Training with other people gives each person a chance to become more skillful in the use of their bodies and minds, more skillful in discerning the difference between a threat and an irritation, more appreciative of people's strengths and more accepting of their weaknesses. Working together with a group of people toward a common objective is essential for human health. Because we are flooded with media and objects it is easy to lose connection with this need. We seek refuge in television, air conditioning, computers, and cars, and forget they isolate us. We have to make conscious effort to recover what we human beings really need.

When Zen master Dogen returned to Japan from China, bringing Zen to the Japanese people for the first time, he said: "I have returned home with empty hands." In those days it was customary for monks returning from China to bring back trunk loads of stuff: scriptures, ritual implements, esoteric paintings and so on. Dogen returned with empty hands. No stuff. Only what people really needed: authentic practice.

65. Rigorous Reflection

Rigorous reflection is required for the alchemy of action to work. It is possible for everyone to be happier. But it takes both reflection (to know what to do) and action (to do it.)

In fighting if you hesitate you lose. If you anticipate you also lose. Timing must be perfect. At the moment of action you must rely on your training. At that decisive moment thinking is too slow. At that moment undertrained people plan. Untrained people panic. But during training we have time to develop in two ways. These two kinds of training converge as the skillful, spontaneous response of a master. One is developing technique. The second is developing samadhi.

Samadhi is the ability to place your mind where you want it. With practice you can keep it on whatever you want for as long as you want. Untrained, our minds tend to wander. In a beginner class, repeating a move or a kata a few times, most people's minds wander away in seconds. It takes effort to bring the mind back to the task at hand. We make that effort. By repeatedly making that effort we get better at it. Our minds become more stable. If your mind wanders during fighting then you will get hit. This is a strong incentive to keep to the present moment. The more you do it the better you get at it.

As we progress we become more vigilant. On the meditation cushion, without the distraction of activity, in a peaceful environment, with no objects to stimulate our senses or engage our mind, we are free to deepen and refine our samadhi. The urgency of karate training can be imported to seated meditation. The depth of our experience in seated meditation can, with practice, be exported into action. This is one way in which action and reflection function not as two separate things but inseparable poles of one practice.

Together they make practice into a kind of gyroscope for life. No matter how quickly the outer ring of a gyroscope spins there will remain a point at the center of the gyroscope that is completely still. A gyroscope on a submarine provides stability and orientation for the ship as it travels. If the gyroscope stops spinning, even though absolutely nothing about the still point at its center has changed, the gyroscope will not provide any guidance or stability at all. This is how the stillness of seated meditation and the dynamism of karate together provide guidance and stability for a life of practice.

66. The Contents of the Mysterious Package

Of the two black belts that Sakiyama sent to me, I chose the one that read "Deep Reality Exists In Training the Heart and Mind." It was his teacher's motto. He saw it every day, on a scroll in the alcove in the karate dojo where he practiced as a young man, in the dojo of his teacher, the great karate master Chojun Miyagi.

Its message is: only through training can we realize our potential. Only by training in conduct can we become free from impulse. Only by training in samadhi can we become free from relentless dissatisfaction and desire, from the disturbance of gain and loss. Only by training can we see how things actually exist, and so free ourselves from suffering completely. Karate can help us accomplish this aim. That was why Chojun Miyagi displayed it on his wall, and why his disciple Sakiyama Roshi included it on the black belt he sent to me. That is why I have had it embroidered on every black belt awarded at our dojo since then.

67. Entering the Stream

A belt means nothing in itself. The effort and mastery it represents means a great deal. One time, to make this point, I told a kids' class, "It's not the belt, it's what you do to earn it that matters. Anyone can buy a black belt...."

It was too subtle a point. Before I could finish the sentence they all wanted to know where you could buy one. Many assured me they had money and would like to buy a black belt right away.

By the time people are ready to test for black belt they have the stamina it takes to practice outdoors in winter in New England all day from before sunrise, in 20 degree weather, to nightfall. Then, on the ice and snow and frozen ground, their training is tested. The confidence they display comes from real accomplishment.

A rank system is a way to help people get started, and to dig in to practice. Ranks help establish clear short-term goals, define a curriculum, and establish a procedure to follow to attain long-term goals. People know what is expected, do the work, and get the results.

After some time, 10, 20 or 30 years, (it is different for each person) the importance of rank should fall away. Instead of months between promotions it is years. By this time the habit of training is well established. Training is no longer something separate from them, some object they take up and use. It is built into their lives. It is something they do as naturally as going to work, or taking care of the people they love. This is the distinction between a student and a practitioner. Practitioners continue to learn for as long as they live, but it is practice itself—not the road ahead—that becomes the centerpiece of their practice life.

At the end of that long day of testing and practice we stretch inside, in the warmth of the dojo. We kneel on the wooden floor. The polished wood feels luxurious. Deep silence surrounds us as we sit. Steam rises from our bodies. Everyone is purified in the heat and sweat of training.

The day the small package arrived from Okinawa unexpectedly, wrapped in brown paper, bearing the return address of Sakiyama Roshi at Kozenji, was the day of a black belt test. Everyone had gone. The test was over by the time I found it in the mailbox.

68. Coming About

Like turning a boat around, when you start practicing you notice a delay between your decision to act and the results. There's an initial elation at finally undertaking what you have always wanted to do. But there is also disappointment. Life still seems mundane and unsatisfying. Only now instead of the pleasant fantasy of what undertaking Zen or karate will do for you some time in the future, how it will change your body, your mind, your whole world, you have the reality of sore legs, feeling clumsy and making mistakes.

This is a point at which a teacher and fellow practitioners are extremely valuable and a book is not. Media can represent experience. They can't substitute for it.

69. In the Stream

We live in a fabricated world. It is filled with representation. Photography, audio recording, designed objects and built environments surround us. It is hard for people living in our time to feel peace, to feel a part of a world and community, to touch the reality of our life. The world we have made is disturbing. Our lives pass quickly.

Instead of a way out we need a way in. Away from the rings of iron mountains. Toward the central axis of our lives.

Every day I and the other people in the dojo take some time to practice kata. Again and again. There we are, and not a drop of sweat wasted. No equipment, no supplies, just people in a place. Simple. Brick and wood. Sunlight, moonlight. It is beautiful. Just action. Imperfect and pure. Our spark of human energy a glint in the endlessness of space and time. Dignity.

Moments seem to begin and end. My human life started, when? Why did it? Dissolving soon, into what? At the very end, there each of us will be. No equipment. No supplies. The living form of our life we feel when, for the first time, we feel the imperative of practice. When we say: I don't want to miss the chance while I have the chance.

70. The Genjo Kata

The word kata means form. The Heart Sutra says form is emptiness, emptiness is form. The choreographed sequence of movements in karate kata appears at first to be a rigidly defined, pre-existing thing. It is not like that. It changes, as you do. It changes you. Your experience of it changes. Kata has existence only as your action.

This is why we can immediately live out the truth in karate that form is emptiness and emptiness is form. Emptiness is not hiding behind form, it is not veiled by form, is not different from form. It really exists, as ours, as us, because what exists is constituted without fixed qualities.

Our whole life, extended in space and time, in body and mind, beyond the limits we assume we have, proves this, and grows from it. We can be free from suffering because of it.

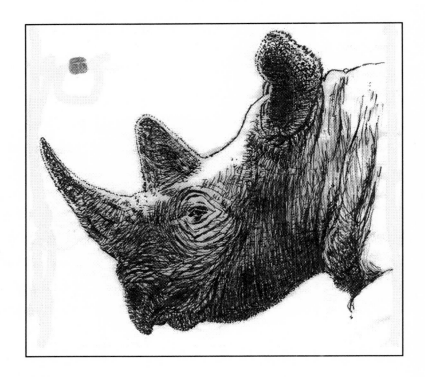

Enlightenment is like the moon reflected on the water. The moon does not get wet, nor is the water disturbed. Although its light is wide and great, the moon is reflected even in a puddle an inch wide. The whole moon and the entire sky are reflected in dewdrops on the grass, or in a single drop of water.

—From the *Shobogenzo*

by Zen Master Dogen

Conclusion:

Why everyone needs a practice

William James in his book, *Varieties of Religious Experience*, quotes a contemporary of his, an Austrian General von Moltke, who wrote: "'Live and let live' is no motto for an army. Contempt for one's own comrades, for the troops of the enemy, and above all, fierce contempt for one's own person, are what war demands from every one. Far better is it for an army to be too savage, too cruel, too barbarous, than to possess too much sentimentality and human reasonableness. If the soldier is to be good for anything as a soldier, he must be exactly the opposite of a reasoning and thinking man. The measure of goodness in him is his possible use in war. War, and even peace, require of the soldier absolutely peculiar standards of morality. The recruit brings with him common moral notions, of which he must seek immediately to get rid. For him victory, success, must be everything. The most barbaric tendencies in men come to life again in war, and for war's uses they are incommensurably good."

James comments: "These words are of course literally true. The immediate aim of the soldier's life is, as General von Moltke said, destruction, and nothing but destruction; and whatever constructions wars result in are remote and non-military. Consequently the soldier cannot train himself to be too feelingless to all those usual sympathies and respects, whether for persons or for things, that make for conservation. Yet the fact remains that war is a school of strenuous life and heroism; and, being in the line of aboriginal instinct, it is the only school that as yet is universally available. But when we ask ourselves whether the wholesale organization of irrationality and crime be our only bulwark against effeminacy, we stand aghast at the thought, and think more kindly of ascetic religion. One hears of the mechanical equivalent of heat. What we need now to discover in the social realm is the moral equivalent of war: something heroic that will speak to men as universally as war does, and yet will be as compatible with their spiritual selves as war has proved itself to be incompatible."

This is precisely the attitude we find in the teaching of eighth century Buddhist Master Shantideva. Writing in the "Guide to the Bodhisattva's Way of Life," twelve centuries before William James, he exhorted the monks at Nalanda University in India to fiercely destroy their enemies without hesitation or mercy. His listeners understood that the enemies to which Shantideva referred were not other human beings, but his listeners' own mental afflictions—the greed, hatred, and ignorance in their own minds that tormented them; and which now hurt us, deform us and may ultimately destroy us.

Shantideva wrote: "These enemies that live in my mind hurt me at their absolute will. It is completely wrong that I should tolerate them and not feel anger for them: My patience with them is a disgrace... They are guards for the prison of the endless cycle of suffering... they are butchers that kill us. How could it ever be possible that I could have happiness, so long as they are living in the net of desire that stays in my mind... I must exert myself, without letting up in my effort for even a moment, until such time as I have directly, and finally, destroyed this enemy...."

He exhorts the monks to exert themselves in their engagement in the moral equivalent of war: "Completely ignoring the pain of being hit, never turn back, never withdraw from the field, until you have achieved your aim...." "You can tie me to a stake and burn me, kill me, you can cut off my head—that would be fine. But I will never in any way submit to my great enemy, the mental afflictions."

Shantideva explains the method for doing battle with the mental afflictions. He details the means, the changing circumstances of the spiritual terrain, the tactics required, and the strategy for the battle, in detail reminiscent of the combat manuals of Clauswitz or Sun Tzu. But his purpose is different.

When the civil war era ended in 17th century in Japan the samurai class fell into a crisis of purpose. Periodically the samurai sought to regain their sense of purpose and their cultural dominance—through attempted coup d'etat or foreign aggression. Samurai who once were supported by the labor of farmers, who spent their time honing their martial skills now were asked to use their skills not for battle but for administration and business. Some had no other way to earn a living, so they taught martial arts to children of former samurai families. But with society at peace came a sense of decline. Strength, courage, skill meant nothing. Dueling was destructive and was suppressed. What to do with their superb skills and well-trained spirit? How could these strong people continue to be of value? How can we? What is the relevance of the warrior ideal, in time of peace or of struggle?

Having a practice provides us with an ideal toward which to strive and against which we can measure our lives. To change our condition in the right way we need a daily practice that requires us to strive diligently and skillfully with our body and mind. We need a practice that allows us consistently to aim our lives toward perfection. We make our lives from what we do. Having a practice directs our energy instead of diffusing it. A practice is a way to polish our spirit for a lifetime instead of accumulating junk.

Our human life needs a practice. For some people it will be work, for others family life, gardening, tennis, music, or prayer. Everyone can have one.

The urgency, the total engagement, the community of action in the moral equivalent of war, was what I was looking for from martial arts. It was why I had to create a world from my own body, words and mind, make my own mistakes, face the dangers and delights of a life of practice, suffer the losses and enjoy the gains and take none of it as the end. I have been more richly rewarded than I ever imagined I would be.

It is never easy or too late to start.

Searching

Glossary

Abbot—The chief administrator and sometimes the senior teacher in a Zen monastery.

Black Belt—The word is used to describe a person, a level of expertise, or a part of the uniform worn by a karate practitioner who has attained a rank or level of expertise equal to training three to four times a week for about four years. Like earning a high school diploma, it is an important threshold in the education of a practitioner. It usually signifies that one has mastered the basics, is serious about practice and is ready for a deeper level of practice.

Bodhidharma—(470-543 C.E.) An Indian Buddhist monk who traveled to China the fifth century to teach Buddhism. He was the 28th patriarch in the transmission lineage from Shakyamuni, the historical Buddha and is considered the First Patriarch of Zen.

Bodhisattva—A being whose life is dedicated to saving all beings from suffering. A Bodhisattva is the ideal for action in the Mahayana Buddhist traditions. He or she engages in the six perfections of wisdom, progressing by means of the accumulation of merit (virtuous action directed at benefiting beings) and the accumulation of wisdom (insight into the nature of reality) through the ten Bodhisattva levels to total and complete enlightenment of Buddhahood.

Buddha—A being who has put an end to all his or her mental disturbances, has awakened to the true nature of reality, who skillfully and completely helps all beings to the degree to which they can be helped.

Dan Rank—This refers to a 'black belt' rank. The person holding it is called a Yudansha.

Desire—According to Buddhist cosmology human beings live in the Desire Realm. We are driven to seek desirable objects and to get away from undesirable ones. Things that engage our senses of sight, sound, smell, taste, touch and thought are all called 'objects of desire'. We misunderstand the nature of these objects thinking their qualities exist in them objectively, and we fail to realize that they will never satisfy us no matter how much we get.

Dogen Zenji (1200-1253 C.E.)—Zen Master Dogen was a 13th century Japanese Zen master who went to China, experienced deep enlightenment, returned to Japan and founded what has become Soto Zen, a leading sect of Japanese Zen Buddhism.

Dojo—Usually translated as 'training hall' it means 'way-place' and refers to the place at the foot of the bodhi tree where the Buddha meditated and ultimately became enlightened. To those in the martial arts a dojo is a place for study and personal development.

Emptiness, see *Sunyatta*

Enkakuji Temple—Center of Rinzai Zen in Kamakura, Japan, for centuries. A Rinzai Zen temple of the same name was built on Okinawa in 1492, by King Sho Shin.

Enso—A classic symbol used in Zen art to represent the true nature of reality, our nature, beyond form or idea, complete, like infinite sky, all encompassing, lacking nothing, with nothing extra, universal, seamless, like moonlight; a representation of the nature of reality which when perceived directly, is the first view of the end of suffering.

Genjo Koan—The first essay of Dogen Zenji's Shobogenzo. It includes the statement: Enlightenment is like the moon reflected on the water. The moon does not get wet, nor is the water broken. Although its light is wide and great, the moon is reflected even in a puddle an inch wide. The whole moon and the entire sky are reflected in dewdrops on the grass, or even in one drop of water.

Genpo Roshi (1865-1961)—Zen teacher of Sakiyama Roshi, a leading figure in postwar Japanese Zen, taught at Enkakuji Temple in Kamakura.

Hakuin Zenji (1686-1769)—Zen Master Hakuin led the revival of Rinzai Zen in 18th century Japan.

Hara—(Jap.) The center of the body; a reservoir of energy found two inches below the navel. In Chinese: Dan Tien.

The Heart Sutra—a concise Perfection of Wisdom or prajna paramita sutra that is chanted at Zen temples and in ceremonies daily.

Karate—Kara means empty, te means hand. It is the name of a group of empty-handed self-defense methods practiced and taught on the Ryukyu Islands, the largest of which is Okinawa. The character 'kara' meaning empty has a Japanese Buddhist connotation. It was substituted for another character, also pronounced 'kara' which meant T'ang, i.e. 'Chinese'. The change was adopted in the mid-1930s when Okinawa was ruled by the Japanese military.

Karma—Action of body, speech or mind. The word can refer to the results of the action or to the action itself. It also refers to the principle that good results always come from virtuous action and painful results always come from non-virtuous action.

Kata—A karate 'form' or training sequence made up of a pre-set series of self-defense techniques performed by an individual against a set of imaginary opponents. Often practiced by groups of people moving in unison.

Keisaku—An encouragement stick, used in Rinzai Zen to strike meditators on their shoulder muscles to sharpen their attention, with the ancillary effect of releasing tension in the back and shoulder muscles.

Kensho—The term used in Japanese Zen for the practitioner's first sudden realization of the true nature of reality.

Ken Zen Ichi Nyo—"Martial Arts and Zen as One." It was Shoshin Nagamine's motto.

Kiai—A shout used in karate and other martial arts to focus the energy of the body and project it into a target. It is the convergence of energy and intention.

Klesha—Sanskrit word for a mental disturbance

Kozenji Zendo—The name of the temple in Shuri Village, Okinawa, at which Sogen Sakiyama Roshi is Abbot

Matsubayashi Shorin Ryu—The style of Okinawan karate founded by Shoshin Nagamine in the 1940s.

Meijin—and genuine, fully accomplished master practitioner

Nagamine, Shoshin (1907-1997)—Founder of Matsubayashi Shorin Ryu

Nagarjuna (first to second cCentury C.E.)—The Indian Buddhist teacher who revived the profound teachings of the Buddha. He taught the Middle Way School of Buddhism, centered on the teachings and realization of emptiness. The term Middle Way describes the path between the philosophical mistakes of nihilism—thinking that nothing exists and that nothing matters—and self-existence—thinking that a fixed objective reality exists apart from the temporal, spatial and mental conditions upon which it is contingent.

Naihanchi—Literally "clawing the earth from within," it is the name of a special set of karate kata, derived from Chinese Tiger style movement, and incorporating Iron Shirt chi kung technique.

Okinawa—The largest island in the Ryukyu chain. For five centuries a tributary state of China, it has been since 1879 the southernmost prefecture of Japan. It is the source of karate.

Oku Myo Zai Ren Shin—Deep Reality Exists In Training The Heart and Mind. This is written in Chinese characters on the black belts worn on our school. It is the motto of Sogen Sakiyama Roshi's karate teacher, Chojun Miyagi, founder of Goju Ryu.

Prajna paramita—Known as the perfection of wisdom, these are the six actions of a Bodhisattva that lead to his or her total enlightenment and which lead all beings to the end of suffering. They are: the perfection of generosity, the perfection of moral and ethical conduct, the perfection of not getting angry, the perfection of joyful effort in doing good, the perfection of meditation and the perfection of wisdom. It is also the name of a group of sutras that explain sunyatta as the nature of reality. The Heart Sutra is among these.

Purgatory—In Christian mythology an intermediate state after death where souls suffer in atonement for their sins and from which they will ultimately ascend to heaven. I have given that name to the dojo where I trained for a few years, before I opened my own dojo, because that is what it felt like.

Rinzai Zen—A school of Japanese Zen Buddhism which uses the contemplation of koans (Zen enlightenment stories) and face to face teaching with a Zen Master as primary means of training.

Roshi—In Rinzai Zen this is the title of a master who has finished the full curriculum of koan study under the tutelage of an acknowledged master in a given lineage. In Soto Zen it is a respectful title for an older teacher.

Sakiyama, Sogen (b. 1921)—Abbot of Kozenji Zendo, karate student of Goju Ryu founder Chojun Miyagi, Zen teacher of Shoshin Nagamine, with whom the author trained in Okinawa.

Samsara—The endless cycle of suffering in which all beings live until they are liberated from it by means of insight into the nature of reality and the permanent cessation of all mental disturbance.

Sangha—Its meanings include 1. the community of disciples of the historical Buddha, 2. any community of Buddhist practitioners, or 3. all the fully realized Buddhist practitioners in the universe.

Sawaki Roshi (1880-1965)—A great 20th century Japanese Zen Master. He founded Antaiji Zen temple and was the teacher of Uchiyama Roshi among many others.

Six perfections of wisdom—see *prajna paramita*

Shantideva (7th Century C.E.)—Great Indian Buddhist philosopher, meditation master and teacher. Among his works is the *Bodhisattvacharyavatara* or the "Guide to the Bodhisattva's Way of

Life." It is one of the most important books in the Tibetan Buddhist
tradition and teaches how to lead the life of a Bodhisattva and so
attain freedom from suffering for one's self and all beings.

Soen Roshi (1859-1919)—An influential pre-war Japanese Rinzai Zen
master, known to the first generations of American Zen practitioners
as D.T. Suzuki's Zen teacher.

Shorin Ryu Karate—Shaolin Style or Pine Forest Style karate.
Matusbayashi Ryu is a variant pronunciation of this name.

Soto Zen—One of the three main sects of Japanese Zen Buddhism,
founded by Dogen Zenji in the 13th century.

Showa—A formal name for the Japanese Emperor Hirohito and as
is traditional in Japan, the name of the era in which he reigned. The
Showa era began in 1926. Dates, like Showa 23, refer to a number
of years (in this case 23) after the Emperor's accession. Showa 23
approximately corresponds to 1949.

Shugyo—Severe training, using methods in which the practitioners
are pushed beyond their ordinary capacities.

Sumi-e—A traditional Japanese painting style using ink and brushes.

Sunyatta—Emptiness. One of the central insights of Buddhism.
It refers to the fact that phenomena lack any nature of their own
which could exist independent of their causes, their parts, their
name and form, or the karma of the observer who is observing the
phenomenon. The direct perception of sunyatta (as opposed to

an intellectual understanding of it) is also known in Buddhism as 'realization', 'seeing one's true nature', 'insight' and 'wisdom.'

Suzuki, D.T. (1870-1966)—Japanese teacher and scholar whose books and lectures in the 1950s were most influential in initiating the American fascination with Japanese Zen Buddhism.

Uchiyama Roshi (1912-1998)—20th century Zen Master who was abbot of Antaiji temple near Kyoto.

Vinaya—The rules of conduct, especially for monks and nuns, recorded in the Buddhist canon.

Zazen—Literally 'sitting meditation,' it is a principal religious practice in the Japanese Zen Buddhist tradition.

Zen—The word, from the Sanskrit 'dhyana' became in Chinese 'Ch'an' and in Japanse 'Zen.' It means 'meditation.' The Zen tradition traces it roots back at least to Bodhidharma, an Indian Buddhist monk who traveled to China on a teaching mission in the Fifth century A.D. Zen Buddhism was influential in Japan from the 13th century on and was at times the official state religion of the samurai military government of Japan.

Zendo—Zen meditation hall.

Author Biography

Jeffrey Brooks is a writer, and a practitioner of karate and Zen.

He began Zen studies in 1974, began practice at Valley Zendo in Charlemont, Massachusetts in 1990, founded Northampton Zendo in 1994, spent seven years studying the teachings on classical Indian Buddhism presented by Geshe Michael Roach, practiced and corresponded with Sakiyama Sogen, Roshi, Okinawan karate master and Zen Master at Okinawa's Kozenji Zendo, beginning in 1995. Sakiyama Roshi translated Jeffrey Brooks' essay on the practice of Mahayana and Karate and circulated it among the Okinawan Karate and Zen communities in 1996. In 1998 Jeffrey Brooks was ordained by Rev. Issho Fujita in the Japanese Soto Zen tradition.

Jeffrey Brooks' martial arts career began in 1977 in New York City, experimenting with a variety of styles and ultimately choosing Shorin Ryu after several years. He traveled to Okinawa in the 1980s and 90s, where he trained with several of the world's leading karate masters, well-known and obscure, among them Japanese National Treasure, former Okinawan Chief of Police, Nagamine Shoshin, who emphasized the practice of karate and Zen as one.

Jeffrey Brooks currently holds the rank of Seventh Degree Black Belt in traditional Okinawan Shorin Ryu karate. He founded Northampton Karate Dojo in western Massachusetts in 1988. Since then he has offered classes daily, for children and adults, with thousands of participants. A number of black belts promoted at Northampton Karate have opened schools of their own across the United States and in Europe, presenting the unique technical, practical and spiritual approach developed at Northampton Karate.

Jeffrey Brooks received a BA from the State University of New York at Buffalo, and an MFA from New York University's Tisch School of the Arts.

He has written speeches and documentary films for notable people in business and in public life, and for leaders of philanthropic and cultural institutions. He has written columns on martial arts for numerous publications including Black Belt Magazine. His column Zen Mirror appears regularly on FightingArts.com.

His seminars and public lectures on Zen & Martial Arts and Assault Prevention are currently in demand at colleges, universities, community centers and private organizations.

He lives with his family in New England, USA.

Note on The Artwork

The artwork in *Rhinoceros Zen* was done for the book by Tarleton Reynolds Brooks. Other examples of her artwork may be viewed at ***www.northamptonkarate.com / tarleton-art.***

Breinigsville, PA USA
11 January 2011
253109BV00001B/28/A